Informal Leadership, Strategy and Organizational Change

Across the spectrum of organizational operations, workplace interactions have proven to be one of the most difficult activities for leaders to manage effectively, especially during any level of change. In these circumstances, leadership strategies, especially related to change and leadership transition, consistently fail at an alarming rate. Additionally, employee engagement and team collaboration continue to be among the most elusive concepts for those in leadership to master.

This book explores the influence of the informal leader on team member engagement during major change initiative in the organizational paradigm, with a special emphasis on leaders who are new to the team composite. This book examines the role of the informal leader in promoting or hindering team member engagement and organizational citizenship behaviors in change dynamics with a focus on change in the leadership structure and major initiatives. The relationship between the formal and informal leader is explored to assess impact on team interactions and capacity to effectively execute change strategies.

This book provides critical information to aid in organizations achieving long-term success and will be of interest to researchers, academics, and students in the fields of leadership, organizational studies, strategy, and human resource management.

Dr. Brenetia J. Adams-Robinson is President and Chief Executive Officer of Epitome' Consulting Services, Atlanta, Georgia, USA.

Routledge Focus on Business and Management

The fields of business and management have grown exponentially as areas of research and education. This growth presents challenges for readers trying to keep up with the latest important insights. *Routledge Focus on Business and Management* presents small books on big topics and how they intersect with the world of business research.

Individually, each title in the series provides coverage of a key academic topic, whilst collectively, the series forms a comprehensive collection across the business disciplines.

Corporate Governance Models
A Critical Assessment
Marco Mastrodascio

Continuous Improvement Practice in Local Government
Insights from Australia and New Zealand
Matthew Pepper, Oriana Price and Arun Elias

Informal Leadership, Strategy and Organizational Change
The Power of Silent Authority
Dr. Brenetia J. Adams-Robinson

South African Business in China
Navigating Institutions
Dr. Kelly Meng

Privatisation in India
Journey and Challenges
Sudhir Naib

For more information about this series, please visit: www.routledge.com/ Routledge-Focus-on-Business-and-Management/book-series/FBM

Informal Leadership, Strategy and Organizational Change

The Power of Silent Authority

Brenetia J. Adams-Robinson

Routledge
Taylor & Francis Group

NEW YORK AND LONDON

First published 2022
by Routledge
605 Third Avenue, New York, NY 10158

and by Routledge
4 Park Square, Milton Park, Abingdon, Oxon, OX14 4RN

Routledge is an imprint of the Taylor & Francis Group, an informa business

Library of Congress Cataloging-in-Publication Data
Names: Adams-Robinson, Brenetia J., author.
Title: Informal leadership, strategy and organizational change :
    the power of silent authority / Dr. Brenetia J. Adams-Robinson.
Description: New York, NY : Routledge, [2022] | Series: Routledge
    focus on business and management | Includes bibliographical
    references and index.
Identifiers: LCCN 2021045780 (print) | LCCN 2021045781 (ebook) |
    ISBN 9780367334659 (hbk) | ISBN 9781032217833 (pbk) |
    ISBN 9780429319969 (ebk)
Subjects: LCSH: Organizational change. | Leadership. | Organizational
    effectiveness. | Management. | Teams in the workplace.
Classification: LCC HD58.8 .A325 2022 (print) | LCC HD58.8 (ebook) |
    DDC 658.4/06—dc23
LC record available at https://lccn.loc.gov/2021045780
LC ebook record available at https://lccn.loc.gov/2021045781

ISBN: 978-0-367-33465-9 (hbk)
ISBN: 978-1-032-21783-3 (pbk)
ISBN: 978-0-429-31996-9 (ebk)

DOI: 10.4324/9780429319969

Typeset in Times New Roman
by Apex CoVantage, LLC

Contents

Acknowledgments

This book addresses a critical, and often overlooked and undervalued resource, the informal leader, to aid in helping employees in the today's workplace to readily embrace change initiatives. I must give a nod of thanks to those who made this book possible.

Profound appreciation goes to all those selfless staff members from departments who served as study participants and took time to speak to me, sharing their experiences and perceptions of informal leadership impact as well as team interactions and formal leadership change initiatives.

To my doctoral dissertation chair, Dr. Doug DeWitt, thank you for your continual encouragement and wise counsel through the development of my dissertation when at times I was unsure of the exact direction to flow. Additionally, as I was offered the opportunity to publish the dissertation, your mentorship was INVALUABLE in how to convert the language of academia into written dialogue that is engaging for all readers. On those numerous times when I was absolutely stuck in the transition process, your advice range in my spirit and help me move the work forward.

To the wonderful formal leaders who provided your interview feedback concerning the concept of empowered leadership, thank you for your openness and honesty. A special thanks to Dr. Latrice Rollins, who provided interview feedback as well as introduced me to the amazing Routledge Publishing team. I so appreciate you for being such a supportive spiritual sister and for providing such an in-depth perspective on formal leadership postures, concepts, and behaviors.

Special thanks to Twanda Black for your wonderful friendship and providing invaluable feedback based on your public relations expertise related to how the layperson would perceive the book content. Your constant support through this process is so greatly appreciated.

It is my hope that the content of this body of knowledge related to informal leadership impact on change in the workplace will help formal leaders maximize their leadership roles and the success of organizational change initiatives.

Introduction
The Challenge of Workplace Change

Resistance to change is a normal reaction because the average person is accustomed to a consistent pattern of behavior and enjoy the security of what they know. Introducing a change element in their norm evokes feelings of fear, uncertainty, conflicting emotions, and frustration. This level of resistance in the workplace can quickly derail a strategic initiative and cause delays that could impact bottom-line profitability. It is, therefore, critical that formal leaders in the organizational structure address resistance as effectively as possible and engage subordinates to embrace a leader's change objectives. The one truth of leadership success is that a leader's interaction with their employees in the workplace is in direct correlation to the level of trust employees have in the leader and how easily employees embrace leadership directives.

Employees who feel engaged, respected, and valued will perform more proficiently related to achieving organizational success. In times of change, it is imperative that employees not only feel valued for their contributions but also have trust in their leadership in order to fully engage in the change strategy. Therefore, formal leaders must ensure they use all potential resources and strategies to gain employee support of change initiatives as quickly as possible. Unfortunately, research confirms that many leaders do not understand how to tap into all available resources within teams to maximize employee engagement during change initiatives (Bankar & Gankar, 2013; Kutcher, 2013). As a result, these leaders fail to obtain employee buy-in of change goals, resulting in initiatives that are minimally successful or completely fail. Many leaders assume that their formal position alone is all the authority needed to get employees to maximally perform.

One of the most underutilized resources which may exercise significant authority within the team dynamic is the informal leader. When the formal leader is new to the team and seeks to introduce new concepts that impact team operations, implementing change becomes even more challenging. "Informal Leadership and Organizational Change" tackles these dynamics

DOI: 10.4324/9780429319969-1

and provides strategies to help formal leaders manage change in the workplace by understanding the influence of informal leadership authority on employee and team member engagement. The strategies herein help leaders create a solid foundation of leadership success that impacts employee motivation and engagement, team cognition and collaboration, and employee organizational citizenship behaviors (OCBs).

This book explores the influence of the informal leader on team member engagement during major change initiatives in the organizational paradigm, with a special emphasis on leaders who are new to the team composite. Across the spectrum of organizational operations, workplace interactions have proven to be one of the most difficult activities for leaders to manage effectively, especially during any level of change. In these circumstances, leadership strategies are seemingly a hit or miss concept that work with some and fail with others, while employee engagement seems to continually be one of the most elusive concepts for those in leadership to master.

This work examines the role of the informal leader in promoting or hindering employee engagement, team interactions, and OCBs in change dynamics with a focus on change related to major initiatives and leadership transition (Bankar & Gankar, 2013; Kutcher, 2013). The relationship between the formal leader and the informal leader is explored to assess the relational impact on a formal leader's capacity to execute leadership decisions as well as the relational influence on citizenship behaviors during change. The analysis of employees' perceptions of the formal and informal leaders' relationship and the resultant influence on employee productivity and team cohesion provide critical support data on strategies to enhance the change environment in any organizational paradigm.

The strategy used to ensure the applicability of research findings was a qualitative case study. Qualitative research is designed to provide descriptive accounts or behavioral understanding of a given phenomenon (Houghton, Casey, Shaw, & Murphy, 2013). It is most appropriate when the strategy is to describe subjective experiences and when there is limited knowledge concerning the area of study. The quantitative approach was not chosen as it is generally preferred when there is ample data available for quantitative analysis and is generally not a preferred strategy to explore individual perceptions (Creswell, 2013; Hoe & Hoare, 2012). Additionally, a large percentage of quantitative research is focused on conceptualizing findings in concrete numbers or volumes. The existing knowledge gaps and social focus of this study did not make the quantitative approach maximally suitable to provide the data required to achieve study objectives.

Qualitative researchers generally posit that the concept of reality is socially constructed whereas quantitative research speculates that reality is an external and observable concept (Cooper & White, 2012). With the existing gap in research related to informal leadership influence in team dynamic and other associated concepts, the qualitative methodology was deemed the most appropriate strategy for this study (Creswell, 2013; Hoe & Hoare, 2012). The data collection process in quantitative research is focused on obtaining numerical information to facilitate statistical analysis. For qualitative research, data collection involves amassing non-numerical information to reach an understanding of interactive behaviors. Since the research strategy involved collecting non-numerical information, the interview format was determined the best platform for data collection for this study.

The case study design was employed to achieve the objective of this qualitative study. The case study approach is generally purposed to obtain an understanding of the complexities of social phenomena as is applicable for the desired study (Creswell, 2013; Crowe, Cresswell, Robertson, Huby, Avery & Shiekh, 2011: Houghton et al., 2013). Using the case study format for the study objective provides the opportunity to examine, explore, or describe a phenomenon in the environment in which it exists. The case study methodology seeks to comprehend behaviors, attitudes, and beliefs of individuals who willingly share real-life experiences related to a phenomenon. The case study was deemed most applicable as it provided the opportunity to explore and identify trends and patterns of behavior as perceived by team members participating in the study.

The findings of the research analysis are summarized herein with a focus on reviewing research data related to topics that most influence leadership and team effectiveness. To emphasize the application of study outcomes, the concept of empowered leadership is used to best define leaders who realize how to utilize all resources on the team to enhance their formal leadership roles and maximally promote employee engagement. Although a relatively new concept in organizational research, the empowered leadership posture has the greatest potential to understand that informal leaders may not have a formal title or be acknowledged on the organizational chart but are resources that can be a formal leader's greatest asset or worst enemy.

In preparation of this book, a limited interview protocol was facilitated with a small but diverse group of formal leaders who exhibited traits of an empowered leaders to assess how they managed their teams. Additionally, they were asked questions related to their emotional drivers, communication strategies, and decision-making processes in reference to engaging team members to become more vested in performing their responsibilities and achieving organizational goals. This information and data helped clarify the success mindset of leaders in today's global environment and provided a leadership perspective on many of the findings from participants of the research study.

The author, Dr. Brenetia J. Adams-Robinson, is an expert in human capital management, leadership education, and organizational leadership. In an employee or consultant role, she has worked for and with the US military, federal government, state government, city municipalities, educational institutions, medical practices, corporate entities, non-profits, and small entrepreneurial businesses. Through this broad range of experiences, she has witnessed the chaos that can result when certain members of a long-standing team (informal leader) hindered a formal leader's capacity to manifest change with efficiency and minimized disruptions. Through "Informal Leadership and Organizational Change", Dr. Adams-Robinson endeavors to help leaders understand the power and silent authority of informal leadership in the team dynamic in promoting change initiatives for long-term success.

1 The Historical Groundwork

Although the concept and detailed study of informal leadership is a relatively new area of organizational development concentration, the concept of general leadership in the workplace has been intensively studied for over a century. A historic assessment of the development of leadership theory is critical in understanding how the concept of management and leadership has developed through the years (Badshah, 2012). This is an especially important point of understanding during times of change (Bouckenooghe, 2010). Theories have ranged from a complete focus on production and bottom-line profitability and general managerial proficiency, to assuring a comprehensive emphasis on meeting the needs of the individual in the workplace to engage (Bligh, Kohles, & Pillai, 2011).

It is important to understand leadership acumen as it relates to motivating followers to engage to make strategic goals happen for organizational success. Most germinal research suggests that employees are motivated to follow those with whom they have a psychological connection and those they like and respect, termed the likeability factor (Stoltzfus, Stohl, & Seibold, 2011). The concept of leaders who empower employees to tap into their capacity to bring their best to the workplace is relatively new to the purview of leadership research. These leaders are perceived as having the capacity to sustain business viability while exhibiting vision, enthusiasm, motivation, and responsiveness to employee concerns to build a strong foundation of employee engagement that leads to stronger team cohesion and collaboration (Martinez, Kane, Ferris, & Brooks, 2012).

Taylor's Scientific Management Theory

Understanding the influence of various leadership theories is essential to comprehending how a leader's influence can maximize organizational effectiveness through human capital engagement. This is an especially important point of understanding during times of organizational or leadership change.

DOI: 10.4324/9780429319969-2

Thoughts and conceptual ideas concerning the influence of leadership and interpersonal relationships on employee workplace behavior date back to the 1500s (Badshah, 2012; Landis, Hill, & Harvey, 2014). However, structured leadership research began with the work of Frederick Taylor, a mechanical engineer, who sought to apply a scientific approach to maximizing job performance in the early 1900s (Chung, 2013). Known as the Father of Scientific Management, he has been deemed to be one of the first and most prolific management consultants in studying how to maximize job performance in the workplace.

The goal of his concept of scientific management approach was to find the most systematic strategy to perform workplace tasks as efficiently as possible (Chung, 2013; Landis et al., 2014). Disappointed with the level of productivity he observed in the plant where he worked, he was convinced that there was "one best way" to perform the work to improve productivity. Believing that just making people work harder was not the best work strategy, he studied the way individual workers performed each task and how the equipment was being used. In the studies, he and his colleagues initiated efforts to understand how a worker's productivity might be improved by systemic work processes and workplace interactions. They addressed such concepts as worker skill levels, workplace motivation, employee needs versus wants, and intrinsic versus extrinsic rewards.

In his 1909 published work, *The Principles of Scientific Management*, Taylor suggested that by simplifying job design and expectations, productivity would be increased (Chung, 2013; Badshah, 2012). He was a proponent that in all processes there is a one best way to accomplish each task, and it is the responsibility of leadership to identify that process. He also promoted that managers and employees should cooperate in determining the best way to accomplish the task and to reach expected levels of performance. Through these studies, Taylor assessed that successful managers must be able to work with and motivate employees to achieve organizational goals. This was a monumental finding since prior to these studies managers in a plant environment seldom spoke to or interacted with workers.

He further postured that to maximize efficiencies, work must have a clear division of responsibilities, which should be clearly communicated to workers (Chung, 2013; Landis et al., 2014). He suggested that the organization should offer incentives to show employee appreciation for work effort to include providing higher compensation to more successful performers. In encouraging workers to provide input in work processes, he emphasized the need for hierarchy of authority, with the need for managerial oversight to ensure work expectations were met (Badshah, 2012). His work acknowledged that there are gaps between where an organization currently operated and where they wanted to be. That gap is what makes the concept of leadership so difficult.

Follett's Management Theory

One theorist, Mary Parker Follett, provided a strong foundation of research to begin the journey of filling in the gaps. Follett was an American social worker, management theorist, and philosopher in the fields of organizational behavior and group interactions in the workplace (Bathurst & Monin, 2010; Boje & Rosile, 2001). She combined her education in economics, government, law, and philosophy to focus on education, community activism, and human interactions in the public school systems. In her observations of community interactions in school systems, she conceptualized that through community interactions, members could unite to address civic indifference, promote harmony among diverse cultural groups, and create a local framework for integrating different community organizations.

In her 1918 work, *The New State*, Follett defined democracy as *a process of subsisting and surviving in a social arena and not just a set of political activities*, suggesting that interactions within the community provided the key to equity and engagement for community members (Follett Parker, 1918; Tonn, 2003). She suggested that individuals within a community are products of the social processes in which they exist and are continually nourished by interactions within those processes (Boje & Rosile, 2001). This revelation eventually led to her applying the concept to the workplace, assessing that the workplace was also community of social interactions.

Her book identified a number of explanations for her argument but specifically defined elements as applied to workplace interactions (Boje & Rosile, 2001; Tonn, 2003). She suggested that the determinations and strength of a group are not disconnected processes among its members but are the collective expression of desires of individuals within the group. In essence, whatever is observed as a trait of the group is only the manifestation of each group members needs and desires. Additionally, she surmised that any experiences that are deemed significant and enduring within the group can only come through positive and diverse encounters in group interactions, which means that group interactions will determine how well the group functions. Finally, she asserted that the individual and the group are not separate concepts from the community at large, supporting that the group's interactions are reflections of the group's overall environment.

These revelations propelled Follett's interest in connecting her concepts in *The New State* to the problems of workplace relationships and management interactions, as defined in her book, *Creative Experience* in 1924, wherein she espoused that her community development theories could equally apply to the workplace (Boje & Rosile, 2001; Tonn, 2003). Organizations, like communities, are a composite of localized social systems involving networks of groups with individuals who bring their individual experiences in promoting group functioning. Through frank and continual interactions with one another in achieving group goals, group members will be able to fulfill their personal goals and strengthen the foundation of group development (Bathurst & Monin, 2010). Although she did not use the term, this is the foundation of the concept of high-performing teams.

She advocated that people were the most valuable commodity within any business operation. She was one of the first to conceptualize the importance of human relationships in the management purview in the industrial sector, suggesting that managers and leaders must view their roles from a holistic perspective and not just in terms of work proficiencies (Boje & Rosile, 2001; Tonn, 2003). She emphasized the need for employee collaboration in management and worker interactions. She was one of the first management theorists to research workplace conflict, suggesting that conflict be conceived as an opportunity for groups to develop innovative strategies rather than be viewed as just a concept to be resolved by individuals (Bathurst & Monin, 2010). This claim earned her a title among some circles as the Mother of Conflict Resolution.

Follett's work aligned with Taylor's *Scientific Management* in that they both encouraged collaborating with the worker on work processes to maximize the organization's capacity to achieve productive outcomes. However, her work contrasted Taylor's premise in that Follett stressed the psychology of human interactions in the workplace with emphasis on including the worker on the actual decision-making process with a focus primarily focused on proficient work output (McGrath & Bates, 2017). His concept did not include the worker on making the decision, only in providing input for consideration of final decision. In Taylor's theory, human capital was still perceived as an extension to proficiency in maximizing machine processes to produce better results. His concept did not suggest that any level of authority was released by the manager. This was in complete contrast to Follett, who emphasized the importance of managers and leaders sharing *power with* workers (co-active power), rather than exercising *power over* workers (coercive power) (Bathurst & Monin, 2010).

Follett and Taylor's work occurred about the same time in history. With the rise of Scientific Management and targeted interest in Taylor's work, reactions to Follett's human relations approach gained less universal support (McGrath & Bates, 2017). After her death, for a period of time interest in her concepts significantly reduced. To some measure because of her gender in a male-dominated industry. However, it was due in large part to the fact that she never actually worked in an industrial setting, and that she proposed sharing authority with workers, which was not a concept that was widely accepted. As the human relations era birthed more theorist seeking to understand employee engagement, Follett's work began to emerge as research of importance and significance. In this emergence, she is now known as the Mother of Modern Management and as the Prophet of Management (Bathurst & Monin, 2010).

Filling the Leadership Gaps

Taylor's work progressed to the human relations era with the advent of the Hawthorne Studies (Hassard, 2012). These studies, conducted from 1927 to 1932, changed the way organizations perceived what impacted productivity, motivation, and employee satisfaction in the workplace. The Hawthorne Study results indicated that job performance was directly related to employee attitudes in the workplace, to include having a sense of value, having the resources needed to perform expected tasks, and feeling some element of control over the work purview. The findings, which became known as the Hawthorne Effect, suggested employee performance is proportional to how they feel about their value to the organization and to their manager. The study was the first to provide analytical evidence that informal work groups impacted the work environment with a focus on social relationship in the workplace and group productivity (Badshah, 2012; Hassard, 2012).

Subsequent to these studies, many scientists and theorists sought to find answers to maximize employee engagement as well as proficiency in work productivity. As time progressed, Follett's work resurfaced and gained traction. Behavioral scientists such as psychology professor, Abraham Maslow, and social psychologist, Douglas McGregor, incorporated Taylor's and Follett's concept in their research to advance the understanding of the human dynamic in the workplace (Badshah, 2012; McGrath & Bates, 2017; Muo, 2013). More researchers then sought to validate and identify strategies to enhance human interactions for workplace success.

Early research studies support that the workplace has many facets that will impact how employees work as well as the role of leadership in how employees perform (McGrath. & Bates, 2017). If employees are not managed effectively, performance efforts will be far less than necessary to meet strategic objectives. To maximize employee engagement, employees must feel they are appreciated in the workplace and feel confident in their leadership and in their leader's competencies (Bankar & Gankar, 2013; Kutcher, 2013; Nasomboon, 2014; Wang & Hsieh, 2013). If employees have no confidence in leadership and feel no perception of value, as followers, they will be overtly critical and may seek to undermine and disrupt a leader's goals. Thus, in an effort to maintain an equitable balance, leaders must be aware of how they approach the leadership role and how leadership actions affect employees Cunliffe & Eriksen, 2011).

Leadership and Employee Motivation

Regardless of the organizational venue, all leaders understand that human resources are essential to the success of organizational goals. These resources are the key to effectiveness, productivity, and bottom-line profitability. According to statistics on workplace engagement, the average employee only gives employers 30% to 35% of total possible effort in a given workday (Autry, 2019). That should be a wake-up call to anyone in a leadership position who understands the impact of effort on productivity. Similar statistics suggest that 80% of employees could perform significantly better if they simply wanted to; 70% of staff are less motivated today than they used to be; and 50% only put enough effort into their work to keep their jobs (Autry, 2019).

With extensive HR background, my experience supports that most employees in the workplace want to enjoy their work and do a good job. They want to be considered a valued resource for the work that they do to achieve set goals (van Knippenberg, 2011). However, the actual output that employees put forth on the job depends upon leaders ensuring that the right foundation exists to promote employees to want to achieve that level of productivity. Research on employee motivation supports that employees are motivated to follow leaders that they like and have a psychological connection based on trust (Stoltzfus et al., 2011). The foundation of such a connection begins with the leader's posture in leading the team.

Leadership Styles Illuminated

Studies consistently confirm that the style of leadership is a key component to establishing an effective workplace relationship with team members (Bligh et al., 2011; Simonet & Tett, 2013). Management gurus have identified several leadership styles, from a very classical autocratic approach to a more engaging approaches (Busse, 2014; Landis et al., 2014; Northouse, 2018). Without effective leadership, organizations would not be able to survive long term in today's diverse, competitive environment. The problem is that ineffective can be just as destructive as no leadership. Some people are natural born leaders; others must seek development to master effective leadership strategy (Ruggieri & Abbate, 2013).

The concept of the posture of leadership has undergone a revolution in how leadership is perceived and the impact various styles have on team member motivation and engagement (Landis et al., 2014). The style of leadership that an individual embraces also defines how much they allow subordinates to influence team operations and listen to team member input (Ruggieri & Abbate, 2013). Some styles inherently resist acknowledging that anyone other than the leader has any influence on what happens within the team. Other styles acknowledge that their authority is not the only influential authority on the team.

With the control and power of formal leadership comes immense responsibility to those they govern (Busse, 2014; Badshah, 2012). As such, leaders can do enormous damage to employee morale and motivation if leaders misuse that authority, either through lack of concern or for lack of knowledge (Bligh et al., 2011; Simonet & Tett, 2013). Leaders have an inherent responsibility to use their authority wisely and strategically to create an environment in which subordinates have an intrinsic desire to achieve set goals. Traditional leaders are less likely to be successful in today's current workplace. Research supports that in today's environment, successful leaders are described as those who are visionaries, innovators, strategic thinkers, intrinsic motivators, and as individuals who do what is right for the organization as well as their employees in an effort to achieve set goals with minimum resistance (Badshah, 2012; Landis et al., 2014; Nasomboon, 2014).

In one research study, it was surmised that true leadership is a choice (Busse, 2014). Unfortunately, many formal leaders never consciously make a choice concerning the leadership posture they will assume. Rather they go with the flow of the environment in which they exist. Historian and leadership professor, James MacGregor Burns, is credited with understanding the influence of transactional and transformational leadership styles on employee performance (Lewin, Hlupic, & Walton, 2010; Zhang, Avery, Bergsteiner, & More, 2014). These leadership styles are the two most prevalent concepts of leadership in organizational research. Burns' research supports that transactional leadership was aligned with the concept of managerial leadership and transformational leadership embodied a foundation of engagement.

Time has proven that not every style is inherently bad (Busse, 2014; Landis et al., 2014; Northouse, 2018). Even the aggressive and less desirable styles have their advantages in specific situations. An individual's leadership style is critical in assessing the influence of leadership style on employee motivation, the capacity for team members to feel empowered and the ability to accept other foundations of influence. To more aptly understand the impact of various leadership styles, following are a summary of the more commonly practiced styles outlining how they are exemplified, when they are most effective, and how they view team member engagement.

Transactional Leadership

Transactional leadership describes a posture focused on the process-oriented exchange between leaders and followers, rather than relationships (Badshah, 2012; Landis et al., 2014). This leader values order with an emphasis on following policies, procedures, and protocols (Arthur & Hardy, 2014; Hernandez, Eberly, Avolio, & Johnson, 2011; Lewin et al., 2010). They tend to be inflexible, risk averse, and not proponents of change. When it comes to interacting with subordinates, they view workplace interactions solely as a function of assuring workplace effectiveness. Transactional leadership is best described as unyielding, rational, and rigid whereby leaders expect a defined level of performance from employees in exchange for a value item, such as salary, reward, and bonuses. This leadership posture focuses on goal accomplishment of defined tasks through structured exchanges between the leader and followers.

Transactional leaders depend strongly on their formal power to achieve goals and seldom consider relationship building in their positions (Arthur & Hardy, 2014; Hernandez et al., 2011; Lewin et al., 2010). They tend to be somewhat condescending in their decision-making and communication strategy, which has been defined as ontological arrogance. Ontologically arrogance is an attitude of definitive, unquestionable knowledge concerning one's position and area of expertise in which they expect little opposition. In leadership, this attitude undermines any potential for employee engagement and does not invite creativity in job performance (Kutcher, 2013; Zhang et al., 2014).

This leadership style is based on traditional management expectation in which managers seek to maintain control with an expectation that subordinates do as instructed (Landis et al., 2014; Lewin et al., 2010). They do not seek to invest in employees as individuals, since staff development to achieve personal goals is not a consideration in the workplace. This leadership posture can create discord within the team, especially when employees feel they have more to offer than just performing the tenants of the job description.

Feedback from the formal leader surveys conducted for this work supported that some of the worst experiences these leaders had were working for leaders who did not communicate, refused to develop them, and made them feel devalued. The transactional leaders with whom they interacted made them second guess themselves, their capabilities, their confidence, as well as their potential as future leaders. Because of the bad experiences with these transactional leaders, the survey participants stated that they were more determined to provide the opposite experiences for individuals that they now lead.

Although positive aspects to this leadership posture will be short-term for most organizations, there are limited advantages to promoting employee engagement in some instances (Badshah, 2012; Kutcher, 2013; Zhang et al., 2014). When subordinates are willing to follow directions and do as instructed, they will be rewarded and have potential to be successful in task performance. It also assures outlined structure in organizations in which such structure is critical for goal accomplishment. This style is best suited in organizations that require disciplined regimens to foresee success, such as the military, some federal agencies, first responders, and policing organizations (Lewin et al., 2010). Practiced styles include autocratic (a.k.a. authoritarian) and bureaucratic leadership.

Autocratic/Authoritarian Leadership

The terms autocratic and authoritarian are generally used interchangeably as there is little to no difference in actual execution and interactions with subordinates. Individuals who are autocratic or authoritarian manage their teams with a mindset of absolute control and pride themselves on their capacity to be decisive and handle problems head on (Bass, 2008; Cunningham, Salomone, & Wielgus, 2015; Kanwal, Lodhi, & Kashif, 2019). These leaders very seldom invite or allow employees to give any input in team activities or decision-making, having little trust in employee capabilities. They believe that they are ideally situated to decide what is best and are often naysayers of suggestions made by others, especially subordinates. In cases of employee pushback, threats and punishment are used to gain employee compliance. They tend to be more blame-oriented than solution-driven. This style of leadership produces a high level of resistance and has resulted in feelings of resentment for leadership.

Although this style is not a long-term desired leadership approach, it does have advantages in defined situations (Bass, 2008; Kanwal et al., 2019). Certain situations may mandate this style in order to effectuate an efficient decision-making process. Acceptable scenarios that generally mandate this more aggressive posture of leadership include crisis situations when decisions need to be made quickly and there is limited time to execute actions, or if a critical project mandates a strictly structured timeline. Individuals who embrace this style as a norm in their interactions will never seek to share any level of authority. Therefore, they would never acknowledge nor engage the influence of an informal leader in the team dynamic.

Bureaucratic Leadership

Bureaucracies operate based on a clear hierarchical structure, tasks specialization, a division of labor, formal rules and procedures, and indifference to personal differences (Bass, 2008; Cunningham et al., 2015). Bureaucratic leadership is focused on managing "by the book" with the book being the book they write. In their effort to maintain control of team dynamics, everything must be facilitated according to stipulated policies and procedures with employee expectations of policy compliance. If the guidelines are not outlined in documented policies or operating procedure, rather than operate outside of documented protocol, they will refer to the chain of command for next steps or approval to deviate. They perceive that their driving role is to ensure and enforce the rules.

This leadership strategy is most effective for tasks that are routine and repetitive, when employees work in dangerous situation, or other highly structured and regulated circumstances (Bass, 2008; Cunningham et al., 2015). Although this leader's intent is to maintain order to ensure maximum proficiency, the results on team interaction can manifest the opposite of what is ultimately desired. This leadership style will generally result in subordinates who only do what is directed out of potential fear of negative leadership responses. Employees will do what is outlined in the job description with very little effort to go above and beyond, initiate any creativity, or think outside the box. In this structure, employees with any level of informal leadership strength will be stifled under leadership expectations.

Transformational Leadership

In contrast to transactional leadership, transformational leadership explores the nature and quality of workplace interactions between leaders and followers (Badshah, 2012; Landis et al., 2014). Transformational leaders focus on cultivating workplace relationships that promote positive interactions to enhance goal accomplishment (Arthur & Hardy, 2014; Hernandez et al., 2011; Lewin et al., 2010). These leaders place emphasis on developing and engaging followers through intellectual stimulation, individualized consideration, and mutual respect. Intellectual stimulation is creating an environment that encourages employee creativity whereby employees stay engaged and focused on achieving organizational goals. Individualized consideration involves the leader being willing to invest in and support the needs of employees, both personally and professionally. Mutual respect involves assuring that employees feel valued, appreciated, and their voice matters.

Transformational leaders seek to connect team members to the organization through the relationship connection (Arthur & Hardy, 2014; Hernandez et al., 2011; Lewin et al., 2010). In today's multicultural workplace, relational competencies have been deemed some of the most challenging and most important leadership skillsets in workplace success. Some of these competencies include employee development, effective change management, maintaining relationships, managing conflict, and negotiating win–win resolutions. These leaders have a strong focus on the organizational vision, are motivators, risk takers, and powerful change agents. Leaders who employ transformational leadership maximize the psychological connection to team members, promote greater follower loyalty, and build a strong foundation of trust (Kahn, 1990; Kirmani, Attiq, Bakari, & Irfan, 2019). Practiced styles include democratic, delegative, or situational.

Democratic/Participative Leadership

The democratic leader encourages team members to be a part of the overall decision-making of team objectives (Bass, 2008; Cunningham et al., 2015; Kanwal et al., 2019). They epitomize the component of transformational leadership that seeks to engage team members in decision to maximize goal achievement. However, they do not focus excessive attention to relationship building and administer their responsibilities in a more impersonal posture.

These leaders are open to listening to input from their team members but retain the right to make final decisions (Bass, 2008; Cunningham et al., 2015; Kanwal et al., 2019). They keep team members informed about all aspects that impact their work purview to ensure shared decision-making and problem-solving. This leadership style acknowledges team member contributions which produces high-quality work, enhanced employee morale, and team collaboration. This strategy is most effective when employees are highly skilled but is not ideal for new team members or staff who require a more hands-on approach from their leaders. These leaders will embrace what others on the team have to say. However, as they maintain decision-making authority, they will likely not embrace a strong informal leader.

Delegative/Permissive Leadership

These leaders take the transformational leadership foundation to the extreme when it comes to cultivating relationships. They are highly relationship-oriented seeking to be seen as a team member rather than team lead (Bass, 2008; Kanwal et al., 2019). Although they will outline desired team outcomes and provide assistance when problems arise, they delegate decision-making to team members. They tend to be overly concerned with pleasing others and have no problem relinquishing their own power and influence to their subordinates. They prefer team members to take the lead in doing what needs to be done without much input from them as team leads. Team members who are work well independently will readily embrace this strategy. However, staff who need more leader engagement will feel undervalued and disconnected.

This style of leadership has pros and cons (Bass, 2008; Kanwal et al., 2019). They are somewhat conflict averse and will seek to minimize having to make demands from team members. However, team interactions always involve diverse personalities and perspectives. As a result, the likelihood of team interactions that are conflict free is unlikely. As such, with conflict averse leadership, team conflict may go unresolved and negatively impact productivity. Acceptable situations to employ this style include situation in which team members' skills exceed the skill level of the leader and they have the competencies to handle the responsibilities without oversight or when highly talented staff would benefit from development through decision-making. As these leaders are not hesitant to relinquish power and authority, a strong informal leader can exert authority with little effort.

Situational Leadership Strategy

Situational leadership generally embodies what transformational leadership involves. They adapt their leadership style to suit the work situations and needs of team members by assessing the individual, the circumstances, and what's needed for success (Bass, 2008; McGrath & Bates, 2017). This leader understands that leadership is not a "one size fits all" situation and not all situations will be subject to the same processes or actions. Execution of this leadership posture will depend upon several factors to include the situation or circumstance; subordinate competencies, personality, and work style; the organization's culture; and organizational resources available.

According to research conducted by leadership strategists, Ken Blanchard and Paul Hersey, a leader who practices this posture will use one of four behavioral approaches to interactions with subordinates, incorporating either a telling, selling, participating, or delegating strategy (Bass, 2008; McGrath & Bates, 2017). Telling strategy is used when team members require close supervision and continual guidance. In this posture, leaders must "tell" team members what is needed when either because they are new or in need of constant oversight. Selling is required when a team member is basically unmotivated and needs encouragement to do what is needed.

The participating strategy is commonly employed when a team member has the competencies to perform whatever task is required but either is unwilling to do so or does not have the confidence to execute (Bass, 2008; McGrath & Bates, 2017). In this strategy, the leader will work in collaboration with the employee to tap into helping them maximize performance. Delegating strategy is used for team members who are competent in doing the job and possess the motivation and drive to do the job well with little to no direct supervision. The situational leader actively monitors the environment and staff to evaluate what is going on and what is needed to assure successful team outcomes. This strategy requires a leader who is willing to relinquish or sacrifice personal glory for the good of the team and the organization. An informal leader will be able to thrive in a team under the purview of this style of leadership.

Empowered Leadership

In today's diverse workplace, leaders who seek to manage solely with a transactional managerial mindset will fail to maximize every opportunity to engage staff for maximum success. When the working population was homogenous with most workers more similar than diverse, transactional leadership strategies were an acceptable norm. However, in today's diverse workplace, the more engaging posture of transformational leadership is mandatory to maximize employee productivity (Hansen, Byrne, & Kiersch, 2014).

Although relatively new as a focused topic of discussion in organizational development, the concept of empowered leadership is grounded in empirical research related to participative management, job enrichment, and delegative decision-making (Speitzer, De Janasz, & Qwinn, 1999). Empowered leaders understand that true power lies in sharing that power with those who are the keys to executing decisions for success. It is defined as a collaborative process that entails a leader sharing their vision of operational excellence while actively engaging team members to own the processes to achieve goals (ASHE, 2006; Speitzer et al., 1999). These leaders seek to establish a psychological connection to empower employees, by helping employees embrace meaning in what they do; that they have competence to perform tasks; that they have autonomy in completing the work (self-determination); and that their contributions impact the overall outcomes. The ultimate goal for this leader is achieving a win–win in team operations, giving employees an opportunity to shine (Boje & Rosile, 2001).

Participants in the leadership survey who exhibited traits of an empowered leader were asked what the concept meant to them. They supported that their primary goal was to lead by example to prepare their team members to achieve personal goals while achieving organizational goals. This aligns with the definition of empowerment leadership (Speitzer et al., 1999). Participants agreed that this leadership posture requires inspiring others to embrace the mission and vision with passion and enthusiasm while letting employees know that influence and authority is not strictly in leadership titles, but team members are valued in the decision-making process. This leadership posture makes it easy for the informal leader to be recognized and acknowledged.

Empowered Leadership Strategies

According to the recent study of empowered leadership, to build the foundation for an engaged workforce, leaders must focus on four critical areas. They also must seek to create a culture of communication, align work with purpose, balance micromanagement, and give team members a decision-making voice (ASHE, 2006; Speitzer et al., 1999). In creating a *culture of communication*, leaders must be perceived as approachable and willing to listen to dissenting views as challenges arise. They must foster a climate of openness and honesty, while ensuring team members realize their value to the team through a consistent and encompassing communication strategy. Empowered leadership helps employees to *align the work* they do with their personal goals and objectives (ASHE, 2006; Speitzer et al., 1999). When employees can align their work with their perceived purpose, the work becomes more meaningful, and they embrace the work with more passion. These leaders must assure clarity of the organization's vision, mission, and core values in helping define team norms.

These leaders must also *balance micromanagement*, assuring they do not seek to micromanage every detail of employee actions (ASHE, 2006; Speitzer et al., 1999). The one challenge of this leadership strategy is these leaders must be consistency mindful of effective governance in assuring compliance to organizational expectations. As a result, empowered leaders seek to help team members feel empowered to work independently, while knowing when micromanagement is needed to achieve set goals. The last strategy is *giving team members a voice* in the decision-making process (ASHE, 2006; Speitzer et al., 1999). Empowered leaders not only value what team members have to say, but they also actively seek to give them a voice, which affirms that their voice matters. By involving team members in decision-making, these leaders support a willingness to listen to ideas which encourages and empowers employees to bring their best to the table and openly invites dissenting views.

Empowered leadership seeks to engage staff through an individualized strategy based on who the employee is and what the employee needs to achieve success in their role (Boje & Rosile, 2001). This strategy involves leading on a level deeper than just the expectation of a paycheck or working in a collaborative environment, it recognizes that if an employee is not connected to the work, they will likely not be connected to giving their best. These leaders empower workers to take pride in their work and to be independent in the performance of their work while engaging in achieving team and organizational goals (Hansen et al., 2014).

Empowered Leadership – Theory X/Y

The concept of empowered leadership is closely correlated to Douglas McGregor's Theory X/Y, based on his groundbreaking work, *The Human Side of Enterprise*. In this theory, McGregor suggested that a manager's attitude and interaction with staff directly impact an employee's motivation as well as their connectivity to their leader (McGregor, 1967). He proposed that there are two polar opposite management postures as it relates to how a leader perceives and addresses staff interactions: Theory X and Theory Y. Both positions accept that a manager's role entails organizing available resources and ensuring that staff must actively work to get the job done (Kopelman, Prottas, & Davis, 2008). However, that is the only common thread that these two leaders share. How they execute getting those tasks done are quite different. Theory X managers are very autocratic and authoritative in their interactions, whereas Theory Y leaders are optimistic in their concept of how employees should be treated.

According to McGregor, Theory X management assumes that workers have a negative attitude about hard work and will seek to avoid it as much as possible (Kopelman et al., 2008; McGregor, 1967). The theory assumes that most of the people are not very intelligent, not very ambitious, don't want responsibility, and have to be directed in order to be successful in getting tasks accomplished. Managers believe that most of the people must be closely monitored, controlled, and coerced into doing what they were hired to do and that the primary source of employee motivation is money and security. As a result, Theory X managers use transactional tactics of command and control to compel staff to work and get tasks accomplished. Intimidation, coercion, implied threats, and micromanagement is a norm in this management posture.

In direct contrast to Theory X, Theory Y management assumes an engaging leadership posture, assessing that most of the people embrace work as a natural part of life (Kopelman et al., 2008; McGregor, 1967). As a result, if the work environment is favorable, accepting a responsibility at work is as natural as play. These managers believe workers are self-directed, reliable, and trustworthy; as such, they do not need to be strictly supervised, controlled, or monitored. They manage staff based on the assumption that employees willingly work for the common good to meet organizational objectives. Theory Y management assesses that if the work environment is positive and supportive, employees will commit to the team and produce high-quality work.

Theory Y leaders believe that employees have a strong capacity for creativity and resourcefulness that can be of great value to the entire organization

(Kopelman et al., 2008). Based on these assumptions, McGregor assessed that the work environment offered great opportunities to align employee's personal goals with organizational objectives. Recognizing that not all employees might thrive under Theory Y management, he affirmed that initially some team members might need some oversight until they develop as seasoned workers (Kopelman et al., 2008; McGregor, 1967). As a result, effective Theory Y leadership incorporates needed supervision for those who need oversight for the time it is needed. These leaders inspire employees to trust, engage, and flourish; whereas Theory X seeks to control and dominate, which results in less trust, less engagement, and lowered staff productivity.

Empowered Leadership Application

In my role as an HR professional, there have been numerous situations in which this theory has been executed in many leadership interactions. In addition to the data from this research study and my experience, invaluable insight was gained from the leadership surveys related to empowered leadership traits in their roles from diverse organizations. The leaders, despite the difference the population they led, agreed that showing value to their staff made a marked difference in the way staff responded in their commitment to the organization. Feedback affirmed that by showing staff they, as leaders, were just as invested in team member growth as in organizational success, employees exhibited more confidence in their capacity to perform, which enhanced organizational commitment.

The leadership results from the survey fully aligned with what participants reported in this study.

Participants generally felt more vested in the goals and objectives of the organization when they felt their leadership trusted them in their role and showed them that they were valued as more than just a body in a seat. They further stated that when they were treated as just a body to get the job done, were criticized, and otherwise treated under the strategy of Theory X, they disconnected not only from the leader but also from the organization.

Theory Y leadership results in employees who feel psychologically empowered (Kopelman et al., 2008). This foundation of empowered leadership leads to employees who believe that their contributions matter and, therefore, are more vested in their behaviors and performance. Empowered employees had more confidence in work output, took more initiative, and exhibited more creativity (Kahn, 1990; Kirmani et al., 2019). This leads to employees who feel psychologically empowered have more trust in their leadership and in their ability to achieve win–win outcomes for the organization and for themselves.

Empowered Leadership and Trust

Trust and its implications in workplace success are a multi-dimensional concept that has been a long-standing topic of interest to scholars (Wang & Hsieh, 2013). It is an employee's capacity to believe that the organization will act in their best interest at all times with the expectation that their trust will not be violated. A strong foundation of trust is needed for employees to feel empowered to give the best of themselves. Employees believe that leaders are obligated to take care of employees and provide for follower workplace needs. When leaders fail in this directive and followers perceive that organizational core values are violated, the trust foundation will be damaged.

In order to maintain a foundation of trust, key critical elements must be exhibited by leaders Sy, 2010). Leaders must exhibit a sincere appreciation for follower's contribution, respect for what each follower brings to the task, caring concern for follower well-being, and be able to remember who followers are as well as promises made (Crossman & Crossman, 2011; van Knippenberg, 2011). Understanding this driving employee need, empowered leaders actively listen to followers to ensure confidence in leadership and don't take employee perceptions personally if employees feel needs are not being met. Maintaining employee trust mandates a level of emotionally intelligence to inspire engaged follower behaviors.

Leadership and Emotional Intelligence

Emotional intelligence, commonly referred to as EI or EQ, has gained a great deal of attention in scholarly circles over the past decade (Cherniss, 2010; Côté, Lopes, Salovey, & Miners, 2010). Although Goleman has been credited with the popularity of the concept, the concept dates back to the 1960s in the field of psychology (McCleskey, 2014). The work of Salovey and Mayer initiated an extensive study of EI, its theoretical influence, and how to measure its effectiveness. Their work posited that exhibiting emotions is not an inherently negative trait. Rather emotions enhanced life experiences and humans exhibited varying levels of capacity to manage emotions, especially in the workplace. The concept has gained momentum within the last decade, with researchers challenging all aspects of the concept's application, especially in workplace dynamics (Côté et al., 2010).

Daniel Goleman purported that one's EI is twice as predictive of leadership success as is the psychological intelligence or intelligence quotient (IQ) (Goleman, 1998). He defined EI as one's capacity to monitor one's emotions and control emotional responses as it relates to actions, thinking, and decision-making. EI is the intrinsic capacity to control one's emotions and to be consciously aware of the emotional climate of those around you (Côté et al., 2010; Goleman, 1998). In a study of leadership capacity and EI, leaders who scored high on EI were more successful in their corporate leadership roles (Cavazotte, Moreno, & Hickmann, 2012). However, there are those in the scientific community who question the validity of EI as a valid concept of leadership ability and its ability to enhance task performance and supervisory capacity. Critics suggested that there is insufficient evidence to support the theoretical implications and practical applications of the construct.

Despite some research questioning of EI validity, the concept has continued to generate massive interest and relevance as it relates to organizational and leadership effectiveness (Cavazotte et al., 2012; Côté et al., 2010). Studies have supported that emotionally intelligent individuals are more capable of the self-regulation and the emotional restraint necessary to achieve success and greater influence (McCleskey, 2014). Emotional intelligent individuals are self-aware, socially aware, self-managed, and relational. Research supports that a leader with lower EI demonstrates negative behaviors that lower employee morale, reduce productivity, increase work absences, and diminish work commitment.

In leadership roles, those with low EI exhibit behaviors to include overblown angry outbursts, display of jealousy of subordinates, leadership arrogance, argumentative, confrontational, uncaring of staff concerns, and blame-orientation. These leaders tend to stand on their positional authority to dominate, control, and belittle staff. This undermines employee's capacity to trust and want to bring their best to the organization as well as stifles innovation and creativity. Leaders with low EI would never acknowledge informal leadership authority in the team relationships. Goleman (1998) assessed that leaders with high EI are more effective in embracing and facilitating change and innovation.

Leadership and Innovation

Some researchers have suggested that effective leadership in today's global, innovative workplace mandates more than strong interpersonal skills or traits characterized by emotional maturity (*Lewin et al.*, 2010; Stoltzfus et al., 2011). Organizations in today's global work environment are continually faced with the challenge of exploiting existing organizational competencies and examining new opportunities for expansion and growth (Muo, 2013). As organizations strategize to adapt to innovation, leaders must possess the capacity to explore and develop innovative ways to maximize existing talent to compete in emerging markets (Cunliffe & Eriksen, 2011). These skills must go beyond analyzing data and managing processes.

Leaders must be able to respond boldly to threats and opportunities without undue or limiting hindrances (van Knippenberg, 2011).

Transactional leaders inhibit employee desires or capacity to exhibit innovation and creativity (Lewin et al., 2010; Zhang et al., 2014). Transformational leadership approaches inspire more innovative employee postures. The empowered and situational leadership approaches specifically seek to inspire employees to think outside the box and present innovative ideas and solutions. To maximize workplace innovation, empowered leaders must be able to inspire employees think creatively and let them know they are open innovative ideas and recommendations.

2 Leadership Engagement Understood

In past leadership actions, transactional leaders operated on the premise that their role was to exert power over subordinates to get the job done. Empowered leaders realize that the most effective strategy to engage team members to do their jobs is not through threats and fear, understanding the critical importance of engaging team members to create a foundation of value and achieve buy-in to accomplish organizational goals. Leaders have consistently faced challenges obtaining employee buy-in concerning change initiatives.

Change in the workplace is a consistent source of frustration, fear, and demotivation among team members (Hashim, 2013). This can result in team member resistance to change initiatives, especially related to a new formal leader's authority and team member engagement (Bankar & Gankar, 2013). It is, therefore, imperative that leaders engage team member to accept change within organizational operations as expeditiously as possible.

The Engagement Paradox

The primary reasons that employee engagement is so crucial in today's workplace are because of the multi-generational and multicultural composite. Prior to our current age of workplace innovations, the workforce was primarily homogeneous, with most workers being male with similar cultural and racial mix. This paradigm made managing the workforce an easier task than leaders must face today. The formal leader had all authority to make all decisions related to what transpired during the workday. When management spoke, workers obeyed, no questions asked. Although many managers in today's workforce try to hold onto such outdated managerial practices, that perspective must shift in today's marketplace if leaders truly seek to engage employees for long-term organizational success (Bhuvanaiah & Raya, 2014).

DOI: 10.4324/9780429319969-3

Engagement Defined

Employee engagement is a critical concept in the multifaceted workplace which seeks to understand and describe all aspects of the relationship between an organization and its employees (Kutcher, 2013; Zhang et al., 2014). The goal is to create a culture in which employees feel valued for the contributions they make to the team and the organization. Engaged employees are defined as those who are psychologically and emotionally invested in their positions, their work, and in the contributions they make to the overall success of the organization (Kahn, 1990). In a nutshell, engaged employees bring the best of themselves to work for the good of organization as well as themselves.

Laying a foundation for true engagement creates a culture in which employees work for more than just a paycheck. In an engaged culture, employees embrace and share corporate values, believe in what the organization stands for, and feel fully integrated in the team (Bhuvanaiah & Raya, 2014). They will actively contribute to creating a positive work environment where employees know they are as valuable to organization as are the hierarchical leaders. Highly motivated, engaged staff have a deeper commitment and loyalty to the organization and consistently go above and beyond to achieve set goals and objectives. Loyal employees stay in positions longer, resist competitive job offers, are easily retained, and actively promote place of work. Creating committed, loyal employees is one of the greatest challenges facing leaders today.

Psychologist William Kahn has been identified as the Father of Workplace Engagement. In his research, he identified three different types of engagement to include cognitive, emotional, and physical engagement (Kahn, 1990). *Cognitive engagement* transpires when an employee fully understands the organization's vision, mission, and objectives. This level of engagement is strengthened when employee know what they need to do and how best to do it to help achieve set goals. The more cognitively engaged staff are, the more they will engage in finding creative solution to workplace problems and challenges. At this level of engagement, employees perceive that their work is meaningful, what they do matters, and that the time and energy they expend to do the work are worth the effort.

Emotional engagement occurs when an employee experiences a deep, genuine connection to their organization (Kahn, 1990). An emotionally engaged employee not only understands but also believes in the values of the organization. It is important to them to feel they are a part of organizational family. As a result, they strive to build and maintain good working relationships with leaders, coworkers, and team member. They desire to work in a positive work culture in which they feel appreciated for that they do for the organization. At this level of engagement, employees feel safe in expressing themselves and their ideas without fear.

Physical engagement is focused on how much physical and mental energy an employee is willing to exert in performing their job responsibilities (Kahn, 1990). Employees gage this level based on how the organization has responded to their cognitive and emotional engagement needs. If the employee is cognitively and emotionally engaged, physical engagement will follow. The stronger the physical engagement, the more fervently an employee will invest in carryout out their required tasks. They will have more confidence in their capacity to perform and give the organization what is needed to help achieve goals. At this level of engagement, employees are confident in their mental and physical capacity to do the job and are happy to bring the best of themselves to any task without feeling drained, depleted, or unappreciated.

Kahn posited that for employees to be fully engaged, all three engagement levels must be present for employees to feel that their needs are being met in the workplace and that they matter to the organizational whole (Kahn, 1990). They will be more vested in the organization and in helping achieve strategic goals as well as embracing needed change to make any goal happen. Fully engaged employees are confident that whatever is needed from them is worth the extra effort to give. Full engagement is a level of psychological connection that is an unspoken bond between the employee, the leader, and the organization (Kahn, 1990; Kirmani et al., 2019).

Kahn explained that employee engagement is not a static or permanent state of mind (Kahn, 1990). Employees might experience different levels of engagement at different times based on the engagement type they perceive is or is not being met. Employees might also become disengaged at any time if the leadership changes, something disruptive occurs in the culture, or something happens to make them devalued. Likewise, an employee who was initially disengaged can become strongly engaged if situations change to meet the cognitive, emotional, or physical engagement need.

Engagement Disconnect

Unfortunately, most of the organizations are not managing internal processes or ensuring leadership competencies to build a foundation for ensuring employee engagement (Bhuvanaiah & Raya, 2014; Zhang et al., 2014). Several actions and behaviors that are regularly practiced in the workplace align to keep a disconnect in employee engagement. Many leaders continue to discount the critical value of employee engagement and fail to realize that their actions could be the cause of employee misbehavior, low performance, team conflict, as well as change resistance. Even those who realize its impact on organizational success, often approach employee engagement in a hit-or-miss fashion.

The most pressing actions that lead to disengagement include failure to make employees feel appreciated for what they do; failure to promote a positive, affirming work environment; failure to include employees in any level of decision discussions; failure to effectively communicate critical information; and failure to recognize employee or team contributions (Bhuvanaiah & Raya, 2014; Kahn, 1990; Nasomboon, 2014). To create a climate of engagement, empowered leaders must assure the organization provides for a foundation for employee value and appreciation, career progression, advancement opportunities, employee recognition and make employees feel safe in expressing themselves. In order for employee engagement to be a cultural norm in the organization, it is mandatory that formal leaders understand what employees need in the workplace and that they embrace the diverse composite of workers in today's global environment (Kutcher, 2013; Smith, 2010).

The Need Construct

Many employers tend to believe that as long as employees receive equitable compensation, there should be no complaints. However, the definition of employee engagement assesses that employees are maximally engaged when their psychological and emotional needs are met to enhance the employee's sense of value (Bhuvanaiah & Raya, 2014; Kahn, 1990). That supports that the concept of engagement is not about money but is benchmarked in what drives employees to willingly give their best.

Psychologist, David McClelland's Acquired Needs Theory has been identified as the foremost theory on understanding what drives workplace behavior. McClelland identified three dominant motivating drivers to include the need for achievement, need for affiliation, and need for power (Bass, 2008; McGrath & Bates, 2017). He assessed that all employees will have all three to some degree, but one is the identified dominant motivator. The identified dominant motivator is a product of an employee's learned behavior, cultural relationships, and life experiences. Once a leader understands the dominant motivator of each subordinate, this will provide the knowledge needed to better meet employee needs to maximize engagement. The dominant motivator is also an indicator of an employee's capacity for a strong posture of informal leadership in the team dynamic.

Individuals whose dominant motivator is *achievement* have a need to set and accomplish challenging goals (Bass, 2008; McGrath & Bates, 2017). They embrace and will boldly take calculated risks to accomplish goals that are important to them. They need regular feedback on how they are progressing to support that their efforts make an impact. Likewise, they want to be acknowledged and recognized for what they do. Because they are driven to succeed, they often prefer to work alone and are driven to keep going when they see the potential to be successful. Individuals with this level of need are prone to speak bold confidence when discussion concerns are related to their expertise. They are likely to fully engage as an informal leader role when the action will be in their interest, and less likely if the action will not enhance their potential for achievement or to be recognized.

Those with an *affiliation* need have a desire to belong to a cohesive group or team (Bass, 2008; McGrath & Bates, 2017). They are generally driven by a strong sense of faith, have a strong desire to be liked, and need to find meaning in their work. They feel value in accomplishing a goal but less about achievement and more about seeing the whole positively benefit. They don't like confrontation and will often go along with the group's consensus to avoid conflict situations. They avoid high-risk situations and uncertainty, preferring collaboration over competition. They see their work environment as part of their extended family and find security in a cohesive work group. Individuals with this level of need are prone to align with the status quo. As a result, they are less likely to assume the role of an informal leader.

Individuals who are motivated by *power* have a need to control situations that impact their existence and seek to influence others to their way of thinking (Bass, 2008; McGrath & Bates, 2017). They desire to have autonomy over their purview of work with the ability to influence the behavior and actions related to that area. They can be demanding and forceful in getting their point across and enjoy competition and winning. They like to be in the limelight, at the center of whatever is going on. They are status driven and seek recognition. They are highly motivated and will generally be very successful with high visibility projects or serving in positions of power and authority. Individuals with this level of need are prone to be outspoken on most issues. As a result, they are likely to easily assume an informal leader role and take the lead without hesitation.

In the workplace, employees have a need to feel a sense of value and appreciation in order to maximally performed assigned responsibilities (Kutcher, 2013). Organizations consistently support the need for highly motivated employees. However, until leaders fully understand the foundation of motivation related to engagement, they will be unable to align organizational goals with employee needs and achieve maximum employee engagement.

Leadership Mindset

I have observed many instances of new leader's dominant entry to the team cause discord and division in the team dynamic. I have worked with and been on teams in which the new leader came on board with an attitude seemingly to ensure that everyone was clear on who had ultimate authority. These leaders were very good at making sure that anyone who did not fully agree with what they said was put soundly in their place. Team members endured the leader making decisions and demands without seeking any input from the team, then finding reasons to blame team members, when a directive or initiative failed or was proved incorrect. Such negative interactions impacted every level of work, resulting in major team discord, lowered productivity, team member demotivation, and high turnover.

When leaders fail to treat employees with respect or treat them in an aggressive, belittling manner, it undermines the entire foundation of the team as well as team members' desires to work to achieve team goals (Hansen et al., 2014). A recent poll confirm that more than 85% of today's workforce have some level of discontent with where they work (Autry, 2019). The primary reason employees leave their organization is not because of their job or salary but because of their leaders (Hansen et al., 2014).

New Leadership Shift

Although a universal definition of leadership may never be agreed upon, there is little debate concerning a leader's actions and behaviors can quickly undermine employee motivation and directly influence the success or failure of team goals (Busse, 2014; Badshah, 2012). Since leadership actions are essential to achieving the set goals, it is important for new leaders to understand the impact of motivation on performance of followers to make strategic goals happen.

Much of the existing theory on leadership transition or organizational change focuses on effective formal leadership and leadership processes at the individual, team, or organizational level. However, there is a critical shortage of research on understanding the influence of informal leadership paradigm on team member engagement of new leaders in the team composite. In the field of HR, we observe many circumstances in which a new formal leader's entry on the team has been undermined by an informal leader.

Leadership can be difficult at any level of team operations, but new leaders must critically understand that a posture of engagement is essential when assuming a new leadership role. They must employ strategies to build a strong foundation from day one or risk being rejected as the team lead. In order to maximize the potential for acceptance of the transition, a new leader must be strategic in making the right impression of team members. A "my way or the highway" mentality will undermine the potential for team acceptance or positive engagement. A prudent new leader must seek to assess the team dynamic before posturing in authority. This includes assessing who has what level of influence on team members and assuring care in the perception they make on employees. New leaders must be mindful of how employees perceive every action they take as they assume the team lead role.

The Perception Paradigm

There is an axiom that perception is reality to he who perceives. Generally, when there is a disconnect between what a leader says or does and how it is interpreted by employees, leaders will often respond "that's not what was meant", "they shouldn't see it that way", "they took it too personally", or any other justification that takes them off the hook. In such situations, I have often had to explain to leaders that an individual's perception is their truth, and, as a result, they will react or respond based on those perceptions. Some leaders get it, listen, and employ more care in how they act or present information. Others insist on standing their ground, ignore the impact of employee perceptions, and the discord continues.

The concept of perception is a key factor in how employees process how they feel about workplace and the value of their leadership (Rego, Ribeiro, & Cunha, 2010; Richards, 1976). When employees perceive the organization and their leader positively, they are more likely to trust the leader, support organizational goals, and remain with the organization over a longer period of time. If employees have negative perceptions, skilled and highly qualified employees are more prone to disengage, disconnect, and seek other employment opportunities, while those who remain will give minimum effort. Some of the most prevalent factors that impact employee perceptions in the workplace include leadership interaction, team collaboration, workplace communication, policies and procedures, and working conditions. Thus, the prudent leader cannot afford to discount the influence of employee perception in workplace interactions.

The Psychology of Perception

German scientist, Wilhelm Wundt, is credited as being the Father of Modern Psychology. He was the first scientist to take a scientific approach to the study of human behavior (Rego, Ribeiro & Cunha (2010); Richards, 1976). In the process of his research, he initiated the study of how the human mind process their environment, which is the basis of the study of perception. Since that time, research in human behavior has vastly progressed to include more targeted research in the psychology of perception, which supports that no two people experience and interpret what they experience the same way. People assess visual and auditory cues based on past experiences, feelings, and expectations to interpret and react accordingly.

In today's workplace, one of the major causes of employee turnover is job dissatisfaction (Stebbins & Dent, 2011). This dissatisfaction is generally the result of a disconnect between the way the leader perceives their effectiveness in their leadership role and the way subordinates perceive leadership interactions. Perception is best defined as the way individuals interpret their experiences (Rego et al., 2010). It is the process of the mental translation of messages of one's senses (sight, sound, touch, taste, and smell) to make sense of one's environment. People will base their actions, behaviors, and responses on how they interpret their reality through their experiences and perceptual system.

Perception in the Workplace

There are several fundamental truths concerning the psychology of perception that leaders must embrace in order to fully understand the impact of perception in the workplace (; Rego et al., 2010; Richards, 1976). Most importantly, one's perception is not necessarily impartial or objective. An individual's perception is based on their subjective assessment of their sensory experiences. Leaders must be consistently mindful of how they say and what they say and be open to feedback from employees on their interpretations. It is also important to recognize that every employee will have a unique frame of reference related to internal and external factors that affect their behaviors.

Employee perceptions are driven by interpretations of their experiences and factors that extend deeper than the immediacy of their situation (Rego et al., 2010; Richards, 1976). The most impacting factors include value systems, beliefs, past experiences, and mental attitudes. Additionally, the amount of energy and drive an employee will expend on tasks and responsibilities is directly proportionate to their perception of the importance of the task. If employees do not perceive their work is of value or find it uninterested, the level of effort put forth will be minimal. If it is critical that leaders realize that one of their most important considerations in their leadership role is how employees perceive actions and decisions.

Although there are different ways to explain the perception process, most of the psychologists support two primary ways that perceptions developed in the mind and drive actionsRego et al., 2010). The first process is through sensory stimulation. During this process, an individual experiences something through one of their five senses and connects it to some prior experience. Good or bad past experiences can invoke responses in the present that ignites a subconscious response or reaction.

The second process is a theory that people will find ways to put together information to complete the story if they are only given pieces of the story

(Rego et al., 2010). It is based on the concept that an individual's environment must make sense to them. One example that is often experienced is a coworker who is only given part of the story in a conversation. If the coworker does not provide all details of the story, the employee will fill in the blank with what make sense to them, and "piece" together what they think is mentally logical. This pieced together story will then be embraced as "truth", and the employee will respond and act accordingly.

Leaders must be consistently mindful of how their actions, behaviors, and communication strategy might be perceived or misperceived by employees (Rego et al., 2010). Although a leader will never be able to eliminate misperceptions in the workplace, they have the ultimate responsibility to ensure such perceptions are minimized as much as possible. It is important for new leaders to embrace that as a fundamental "truth" of their initial leadership strategy. If that is not clearly understood, leaders are subject to being the primary cause of employee disengagement due to gross misperceptions of leadership actions, behaviors, or communication.

Managerial Leadership in Execution

The words "leader" and "manager" are among the most commonly used and misunderstood words in the business arena. Although they are often used interchangeably, these are two distinct processes that are both critically needed in the team dynamic to successfully meet the organizational mission (Bârgau, 2015). There has also been much debate on if the transactional leadership mindset still has any significance in today's modern workplace. In an effort to address this question, some researchers have sought to explain leadership in terms of two levels of needed knowledge – management skills and leadership acumen.

It has been assessed that management relates to the overall programmatic and tactical responsibilities, while leadership is focused on influencing human capital in achieving managerial objectives. A proficient leader must be adept at both directives. Strong leadership is needed to ensure a workforce that is engaged, productive, and inspired to align their efforts with organizational goals (Bârgau, 2015). Strong management is needed to assure that activities and processes are developed and followed to maintain an efficient operation.

True Leadership Versus Management

John Kotter, a Harvard University professor and best-selling author, defined the difference between leadership and management based on observed behaviors and tasks (Kotter, 1990b). Kotter argued that leaders and managers perform tasks that are basically converse in nature but are both critical to long-term organizational success. Management is best defined as providing direction in task completion, involving staff developing, employee mentoring for task proficiency, and resolving conflicts within the team environment (Bârgau, 2015; Kotter, 1990b). Managers take care of planning, organizing, budgeting, coordinating, and monitoring team activities for organizational objectives through efficient use of human capital resources. These are all critical tasks that must be facilitated with proficiency in order to ensure programmatic success.

Kotter simplified the concept of management as the positional authority to keep an organization functional (Kotter, 1990b). Proficient managers ensure effectiveness in reaching short-term goals, consistency in minimizing risks, and uniformity in establishing standardized processes for improve outcomes (Bârgau, 2015; Kotter, 1990b). Managers generally focus on adhering to defined guidelines to ensure proficiency in performance to achieve specific outcomes. One management guru surmised that assuring performance proficiency was a tight rope walk in operations in that there must be a balance of efforts in monitoring staff. Over-monitoring employee activities is time consuming and could easily result in demotivation. Under-monitoring could result in unexpected and unwanted surprises. Either paradigm could undermine desired results of proficiency in work outcomes.

According to research by Harvard Professor Robert Katz, proficient managerial success is dependent upon three competency areas: technical, human, and conceptual (Katz, 1955). Technical skills refer to the capacity to proficiently perform tasks in a specific area of work and specialty. Human skills comprise the ability to work with diverse populations to enhance the capacity to effectively assist in task completion. Conceptual skills encompass the aptitude to work with various ideas and employ competencies related to strong communication, organization, negotiation, and delegation. Proficient leaders must possess leadership acumen as well as strong managerial competencies.

Management and Leadership: Clarifying Components

Many management gurus and organizational development authorities have documented and outlined the numerous perceived differences between leadership and management (Bârgau, 2015). In analyzing the various chart variances, the most important differences between the two concepts concern how they view their roles related to human capital and how they approach human interactions in the workplace. The most impacting differences are summarized with experiential observation in Table 2.1 (Bârgau, 2015; Bass, 2008; Kotterman, 2006; Lunenburg, 2011).

Table 2.1 Management Versus Leadership Differences

Processes	Management	Leadership
Focus	• Task-focused • Results and outcomes • The "how", the "when" • Risk averse, certainty	• People-focused • Change, results, and empowerment • The "what", the "why" • Risk taking, possibilities
Prime Directive	• Planning, tactical execution • Developing processes/timelines • Impersonal attitude/posture	• Planning, creative execution • Developing strategy • Passionate attitude/posture
Staff Interaction	• Directing staff to maintain structure • Delegating responsibility • Creating order through processes and procedures • Displays low emotion in staff interactions	• Aligning people skills with organizational needs • Communicating vision • Creating coalitions through inspiration and motivation • Displays high emotion to connect with staff
Vision Execution	• Identifying problems, getting to quick resolution • Directing vision action for staff execution • Instructing staff in overcoming conflict and barriers • Taking low-risk approach to problem resolution	• Discussing problems for problem resolution buy-in • Sharing vision to fully engage staff • Empowering staff to process through conflict barriers • Taking high-risk approach to problem resolution
Vision Outcome	• Monitoring results to ensure conformity • Mandating outcomes aligned with leadership expectations	• Monitoring results with expectation of innovation • Promoting creativity in vision outcomes
Staff Engagement	• Strong emphasis on hierarchical power • Leader is driving power authority in decision-making • Formal authority is the most critical aspect of team operations	• Strong emphasis on engaging each member as part of team • Team members have equal voice in decision-making • All levels of authority and influence are embraced

In daily execution of organizational operations, the most effective leaders must be able to wear both operational hats. The most empowering leaders wear both hats with proficiency to be successful in their leadership role and fully engage those they lead (Bârgau, 2015; Kotterman, 2006; Lunenburg, 2011). Such engagement includes encouraging and allowing team members to freely use their strengths. Tenured and new formal leaders should understand how to interact with staff as proficient leaders with strong managerial competencies with a posture of engagement (Waite, McKinney, Smith-Glasgow, & Meloy, 2014). Leaders must also know how and when to formally engage informal leadership influence to maximize employee engagement, especially in times of change and transition.

3 The Informal Leadership Paradigm

Several years ago, in my capacity as a new HR Manager, a new HR Director was introduced to the team. Because of the psychographics of the appointment, there was much excitement as to the potential for change that was hoped for in this leader's appointment. This was a perceived strong individual in a predominantly like situated demographic organization. There was hope of changing the negativity of the work culture, introducing more levels of diversity, bringing new ideas, and introducing new initiatives. The entire HR team was excited at the possibilities. Then, within six months, the entire team was frustrated, irritated, aggravated, and all the other "ateds" in the dictionary, with many actively seeking other employment opportunities.

The new leader's perception was that their positional authority gave them all authority to speak to staff in any tone they wanted, say things that seemed to intentionally demoralize, and treat those who were clearly informal leaders with the harshest tones of address. They exhibited a very low level of emotional intelligence, which appeared to specifically target anyone who seemed to be informal leaders on the HR team. The intent seemed to be to drive the long tenured and respected staff, who had informal leadership influence, out of the organization so the formal leader would have a stronger power base. In the end, the result was massive demotivation, team division, and failed change initiatives. Additionally, there was substantial turnover and employees who remained tried diligently to avoid any interaction with the formal leader.

Previous research related to leadership provided minimum foundational data concerning the informal leader influence on team dynamics and follower behaviors. Although limited, the little germinal data available support that the informal leader has proven to be a trusted member of the team and has a strong foundation of respect and support (Luria & Berson, 2013; Ng'ambi & Bozalek, 2013). As a result, formal leaders who fail to understand the level of authority that informal leaders might exercise could do great harm to their positional authority as formal leaders as exhibited in the previous scenario. However, there are substantial gaps in research related

DOI: 10.4324/9780429319969-4

to the informal leader's role and influence on workplace behaviors, team engagement, and responses to change initiatives. These gaps need to be addressed in order to help formal leaders engage employees to achieve set goals and objectives.

Why Study Informal Leadership?

The minimal research related to informal leadership supports that change in the workplace would be more successful with the strategic use of informal leaders in the workplace (Downey, Parslow, & Smart, 2011). There is an abundance of existing information and data concerning the need for change in leadership strategy, the impact of change on staff productivity, as well as the effect of organizational citizenship behaviors (OCBs) on change initiatives. However, until recently there has been little substantive research on the authority of the informal leader and the impact of the informal leader's influence on change in the workplace.

Change is in today's work environment is mandatory for continued organizational growth. Although change incites fear, doubt, anxiety, and in many instances anger, effectively managed, there are strategies that may enhance the potential for success (Hashim, 2013). In an effort to minimize the increased level of conflict and discord that change provokes, it is important for leaders to understand how the relationship between the formal and informal leaders influence OCBs in the team environment during the leadership transition. With the massive failure of change initiatives, enhancing this area of knowledge maximizes a leader's capacity to ensure success in maximizing team effectiveness in the midst of change initiatives.

Research concerning informal leadership and informal leader influence is limited as it relates to the workplace and team interactions (Downey et al., 2011; Luria & Berson, 2013). Thus, much of the focus of this discussion is on the few germinal theorists and their research related to the concept of informal leadership theory. Informal leaders are those individuals in the organization who despite holding no formal title are still recognized as leaders (Downey et al., 2011). Much of the information in the aforementioned section on leadership is not directly linked to a formal title or position. Thus, the individual in any position who exhibits certain leadership traits can garner a position of strength, either formally or informally, on the team and in the organization.

Sources of Organizational Power

The word power is often associated with negativity, especially in light of so many ethically borderline mega-business activities that have made headlines in the last decade. However, without the concept of power and all, it entails leaders could not build the foundation for business success. The power bases in today's organization have shifted from positional power to more relational oriented power bases to accommodate the need for a more engaging workforce (Turner & Schabram, 2012). Research suggests that power alone has very little impact and can neither strengthen nor weaken an individual or a situation. When influence is exerted with a strong power base, the subsequent effect will have a significant impact on interpersonal interactions, resulting in an emphatic positive or negative outcome. Personal power bases that inspire team member followership have a much greater impact on workplace productivity than flexing positional power, which can manifest negative outcomes and failed directives (Ng'ambi & Bozalek, 2013; Ross, 2014).

The informal leader is not endowed with formal position power as attributed to the formal leader. However, this leader can exercise enormous influence over team members through other relational and interpersonal group dynamics (Turner & Schabram, 2012). In accordance with the social phenomenon in a work setting as studied by social psychologists, John French and Bertram Raven, power within an organizational environment presents itself in five forms, which includes legitimate, coercive, reward, referent, and expert (French & Raven, 1959; Turner & Schabram, 2012). They later added an additional element to this power base, termed informational power. These power sources are collectively referred to as social power influence.

Legitimate power is derived from a positional authority or by virtue of a set of formal relationships as generally defined by an organizational chart (French & Raven, 1959; Turner & Schabram, 2012). It is simply the formal position held in the organization. Employees will generally comply with individuals with legitimate power and do as they are directed based on organizational expectations that they do so. If and when a subordinate refuse to comply with a directive given, by virtue of the leaders' title, he or she has the power to issue disciplinary action. As a result, if this level of power is the only base the leader has, subordinates comply in order to avoid the action due to the capacity of the leader to exert that level of control.

The leader's base of authority and power is fundamentally rooted in the title they hold based on the governing rules of the organization and the subordinate team member's perception that the leader has authority to exert specified control (French & Raven, 1959; Turner & Schabram, 2012). When the individual no longer has the position, they no longer have authority to wield power over the subordinates. This level of power is the most commonly and easily recognized and accepted source of power in any work culture. It is generally the first thing that comes to mind if one were to ask who is "in charge".

However, when an individual has legitimate authority and assumes that power base gives them ultimate authority, they will have a rude awakening. This power base does not automatically imply a positive relationship with team members, nor that team members will automatically comply with all they instruct them to do (French & Raven, 1959; Turner & Schabram, 2012). The position itself does not automatically grant the titleholder maximum authority, nor does it automatically imply they will be successful as the leader. There are many aspects that can enhance the legitimate leader's positional power or can undermine their effectiveness. This is especially true of new leaders in the team dynamic.

Although the primary advantages of this base of power it is so easily recognized as the power source, there are many disadvantages if the leader is not cognizant to subordinate perceptions or does not have the skill to be successful in the role (French & Raven, 1959; Turner & Schabram, 2012). If the leader does not have the skill needed in the position, the lack of leadership proficiency will quickly be recognized by team members. This will quickly undermine the level of respect that team members exhibit towards the leader and may eventually result in frustration and irritation at the lack of leadership. Holding the title on the team alone does not mean that team members will embrace the person or their authority. Many new and unwise positional leaders come into a team dynamic and just expect to be wholly embraced as the leader. They do not understand that the level of engagement mandates time to build a perception of respect and loyalty.

Coercive power involves the capacity to force someone to do things against their will (French & Raven, 1959; Turner & Schabram, 2012). This usually likewise involves having the ability to punish the individual if they refuse to comply with a directive. Coercive power may be exhibited in a number of ways, to include withholding positive reinforcement, potential for corrective or disciplinary action, threats of potential demotions, and the threat of termination. Unfortunately, such actions could result in levels of resentment and underlying anger if not wielded with caution and wisdom. As a result, new leaders must be very cautious in how they use the authority to dispense coercive power.

Exhibiting coercive power is necessary in some industries more than in others (French & Raven, 1959; Turner & Schabram, 2012). The manufacturing and construction industries must have very strict guidelines in operations due to the high potential for accidents that can be extremely serious or deadly. As a result, guidelines are clear as to resulting actions if certain performance expectations are not met. Industries that are intensively regulated will also have leaders who are endowed with extensive coercive power to ensure that strict guidelines are followed with little deviation, such as banking and medical facilities.

When leaders have the capacity to dispense coercive power, they generally have the ultimate authority to outline performance and behavior expectations (French & Raven, 1959; Turner & Schabram, 2012). There is generally an inherent expectation of compliance without deviation. This is specifically true where the industry has very specific regulatory guidelines, rules and procedures, and legal implications. As with legitimate power, leaders who have this level of authority often expect compliance without deviation. Unfortunately, also like legitimate power holders, this is not always the case.

Advantages of this level of authority are primarily helpful when the team has new, inexperienced, or unmotivated team members (French & Raven, 1959; Turner & Schabram, 2012). This level of power may provide some measure of encouragement for these employees to focus on tasks or learn the skill to minimize the potential for retribution. This power base is also helpful when the organization has a change initiative that requires the team's input to facilitate. When change is the subject of staunch resistance, coercive power can make the difference between a change initiative being stalled and pushing team members to do what's needed, even when they disagree.

Coercive power can also be massively abused if the leader is not experienced or wise in its application (French & Raven, 1959; Turner & Schabram, 2012). Coercive power can be misused by arrogant leaders who met out actions based on pet peeves or emotional upsets. Some leaders dispense coercive actions without regard of team relationships or the impact on team cohesion. This can be especially problematic if the leader does not dispense coercive power decision equitably and fairly. A more unscrupulous leader might threaten coercive action if a team member does not comply with a leader's desires that have little to do with policy or regulatory procedures, such as if a subordinate disagrees with the leader or when the leader has an active dislike of the subordinate.

Reward power is the opposite of coercive power and refers to a leader's ability to inspire subordinates by providing incentives for goal achievement (French & Raven, 1959; Turner & Schabram, 2012). This involves offering benefits to an employee for doing something that is desired or advantageous, especially as it relates to the leadership or the organization. This, like coercion, is achieved when there has been compliance to directives, achievement of performance expectations, or attainment of an organizational goal. A reward may be anything that has perceived value to the employee population or that makes team members feel motivated to engage and produce. Rewards might include promotions, pay increases, bonuses, verbal praise, certificates, and awards.

The concept of motivation, like leadership, has been defined in a number of different ways (French & Raven, 1959; Turner & Schabram, 2012).

The most simplistic understanding of the concept is that motivation is the fundamental reason that prompts an individual to act or behave in a certain way. True motivation is an internal process that provokes or directs one to maintain a desired level of behavior over an extended period of time and is a personal journey for each individual. Leadership excellence mandates the leader creates an environment wherein employees are inspired to tap into their intrinsic motivation to achieve organizational goals.

Reward power, if executed proficiently, can be one of a leader's greatest assets. To ensure it works advantageously, the leader will have to understand each team member's motivation and what makes them feel valued (Stebbins & Dent, 2011). Employees now expect to be rewarded for successfully applying their skills and making a positive contribution to the organization. Leaders who fail to recognize this new workplace dynamics and the motivational impact are setting themselves and the organization up for failure. Understanding employee motivation is crucial to a leader's understanding of how to deploy reward power in the most impacting way.

There is no one size fits all recipe in laying the foundation for employee motivation and making each team member feel they are valued by the leader and the organization (Stebbins & Dent, 2011). Some feel motivated and valued by a simple word of praise to make them feel the leader appreciates them. Some prefer something that can be posted or displayed publicly, such as a framed certificate, a plaque, or a trophy. Some have a need to be acknowledged for their expertise and desire public accolades by inclusion in a special project or leading a special task force. Being a recipient of a reward that satisfies their motivational need inspires employees to feel good about their connection to the leader and the organization, and thereby more commitment to performance and productivity.

If not executed properly, reward power can produce undesired outcomes (French & Raven, 1959; Turner & Schabram, 2012). It may produce a mindset in employees to follow direction, resulting in compliance, but may not inspire commitment. It can also be counter-productive to team camaraderie by enhancing the rewarded staff's ego, which will negatively impact team collaboration and may promote team member jealousy and resentment. It is for these reasons that leaders must fully understand how to implement rewards in the workplace before rollout. This is especially true for those new to the team dynamic.

Referent power is derived from what some call the likeability factor (French & Raven, 1959; Turner & Schabram, 2012). It is the capacity of the leader to influence team members based on the respect, admiration, and connection they have to the leader. It is derived from an individual's capacity to be liked and respected based on the value they are perceived to bring to the team and may also be based on charm and attractiveness. Like expert power, it is not influenced by positional authority. It is not considered one of the strongest sources of power in the workplace.

Referent power is not a formal power base as it is totally based on personal qualities of a leader and his or her ability to have a psychological connection to team members (French & Raven, 1959; Turner & Schabram, 2012). Based on the intrinsic qualities, subordinates grow to admire, trust, and respect, not only the leader's position but also who they are and what they bring to the table. In essence, they grow to genuinely like the leader. As a result, they are more committed to engaging with the leader to achieve whatever goals the leader reveals.

To reference something or someone is to have the deepest respect and honor for that thing or person. It is often the label one puts on a spiritual or divine connection. Referent power has been deemed the most important source of influence a leader can possess (Turner & Schabram, 2012). These leaders consistently earn and maintain the trust of those they lead, which directly influences engagement, productivity, and commitment to the leader and the goals outlined. Research consistently supports that employees do not leave organizations; they leave their leaders. Conversely, they can be completely frustrated with the way the organization operates, but if they are psychologically connected to their leader and their teammates, they will stay or at least tend to stay longer (Stoltzfus et al., 2011).

Referent power is benchmarked in the capacity to listen and hear what team members are saying (French & Raven, 1959; Turner & Schabram, 2012). These leaders are considered great communicators who give the perception that what the individual has to say truly matters. Referent leaders are inspirational and naturally motivational. They are perceived as reliable, dependable, someone a team member can completely depend upon in the trenches. These are the leaders who have no problem sharing the limelight or even stepping back to let a team member shine.

Although this social power source is one of the strongest influential sources in a leadership paradigm, there are some disadvantages of which an empowered leader must be mindful. This power source is rooted in trust, which takes time to develop (Turner & Schabram, 2012). As a result, in work environments with high turnover, referent power does not always have an opportunity to make an impact in the workplace. Secondly, if the culture is strongly negative, a referent power source may be undermined or crushed before the leader can get incepted into the team. A leader may seek to model this inspiring power source, but if the culture does not promote such behavior, it will be difficult to get things done or positively impact. Finally, referent power is not appropriate in crisis situation or when the culture mandates a regimented leadership style. A new formal leader to the team will benefit greatly from seeking to build the foundation for referent power.

Expert power is the source of power derived from an individual's perceived level of expertise in his or her field or within the organization (French & Raven, 1959; Turner & Schabram, 2012). The source may be based on their skill, proficiency, competence, and knowledge that make them a trusted "go to" member of the team and in their ability to influential others. This power source is based on team members' perceptions and beliefs that the leader possesses expertise or enhanced knowledge that team member do not possess. This power base is independent of any formal position within the organization but is specialized knowledge acquired through education or over years of experience in the specialized area. This is the subject matter expert with specializations in human resource management, financial planning, engineering, computer technology, etc.

A key advantage for a leader who is perceived as an expert is that team members will be open to hear what they have to say and will generally trust guidance and advisement that is given by the leader (French & Raven, 1959; Turner & Schabram, 2012). Team members will generally automatically seek input and guidance from he or she who is considered the "expert" in the group. If this is the leader, this foundation makes it easier for the leader to get team members to veer in the direction they desire. Once a leader establishes themselves as an expert, it is easier to build upon the power base and gain a strong level of respect and admiration throughout the organization.

The biggest disadvantage is that this power source can be a two-edged sword (Turner & Schabram, 2012). Once the expert status has been established, more people will come to glean from the leader's knowledge base which highlights the expert power base. However, as the leader shares the knowledge base, it will invariably diminish the leader's power base. This leads to the second disadvantage. In order to retain the thrown as the expert, the leader must constantly work to maintain knowledge and skill level. The third and greatest disadvantage is there is always a potential threat that someone with a greater knowledge base will come on the scene. In such case, the power base may be instantly diminished.

Informational power was added to the concept of social power in the latter years of French and Raven research strategy (Turner & Schabram, 2012). It is defined as the capacity to control information needed by others to reach important organizational goals and decisions (French & Raven, 1959; Turner & Schabram, 2012). This power source is generally based on longevity in the organization which results in a foundation of knowledge and use of information on how to get things done. This influencer is considered to be a strong information resource and have access to information that others do not have or would have difficulty finding out. Although there are similarities between information and expert power, they are different. Information power is based solely on having operational level information to share, generally due to the length of time with the organization. Whereas expert power is based on specialized knowledge and information acquired through education and professional acumen.

This base of power can be one of the strongest foundations of authority in an ever increasing information driven world (French & Raven, 1959; Turner & Schabram, 2012). However, it is also considered a power source that has the potential to be a shorter-term power because it is not based on who the person is but strictly on what the person knows. Information power can be transitory in that the information might be obtain by others who may be better at sharing or conveying it. Additionally, once the information is shared, instantly the power base may be weakened if there is no additional information to share concerning the area in question. Someone might be considered a holder of information power in a crisis situation when certain level of information might be critical to resolving the problem. However, after the crisis ends, the holder of information power may no longer be of great value until a similar crisis occurs.

An additional issue with this power base is that it is not dependent on the character of the power holder (Turner & Schabram, 2012). The one with information power is just the conduit to pass information along. It is possible that the information can be found or obtain from sources outside of the one considered the information broker. Maintaining the status also means that the leader with information power will need to constantly be vigilant about keeping abreast of new sources of information related to the area of specialty. Having information power is not about having one piece of good information; it is a designation given because the individual has proven to be a continual resource of information that is difficult to obtain or difficult to understand.

As a short-term power base, the best way for an individual to capitalize on this level of influence is to be generous in sharing the information in a way people can easily understand to build a reputation as a go-to resource (French & Raven, 1959; Turner & Schabram, 2012). Team members will begin to see this individual as someone who has the best interest of the team at heart. It is critical to avoid using information to undermine or negatively impact the team or the organization but use it as a source of help to the team and the organization. It is important to use the information wisely to build trust and credibility. The key to maintaining information power is to cultivate sources of information flow that others do not possess, ensure it is always accurate, and to share it in a way that people perceive the leader as a key critical cog in an organization's information flow.

Social Power Base Utilized

Unless otherwise granted by organizational culture, legitimate, coercive, and reward power sources fall strictly within the purview of formal leadership authority (French & Raven, 1959; Turner & Schabram, 2012). Informal leadership influence is manifested through one referent, expert, and informational power. Informal leader authority is rooted in the fact that team members connect to the individual on an interpersonal level and acknowledge the informal leader's influence within the team dynamic. Thus, the informal leader with a strong personal power base may, indeed, yield more influence over team members than the positional authority of the formal leader.

According to research conducted by management strategists, John Katzenbach and Zia Khan, on the formal and informal structures in organizations, the informal structure can be more significant than the formal structure because of the close social connection informal influencers have on team members (Khan & Katzenbach, 2007). The concept of empowered leadership involves the capacity to align people with a defined vision and focus on motivating and inspiring others. The capacity to motivate and inspire others has been a key component of how effective informal leadership behavior has in organizations. However, because informal leaders do not have formal authority to rely on in promoting follower action, these leaders must rely on their capacity to connect to and incite others to act, a concept that has been termed authentic leadership (Hernandez et al., 2011).

In the formal leadership survey, when asked how they engaged the informal leaders as new formal team leads, they supported that the most critical action they took initially was not to make any critical decision before observing the team interactions. As engaged leaders, they wanted to first identify the informal leaders; to understand the purview of their level of influence, that is, if their influence was based on their personalities or knowledge base; and finally, to gage how much influence and authority they had on team members. They then intentionally found ways to engage identified informal leaders based on their foundation of influence. These leaders agreed that the worst thing a formal leader could do as a new team lead was to make informal leaders feel devalued and that their presence, knowledge, and influence did not matter.

Authentic Leadership Theory

Authentic leadership theory proposes that leaders have more positive influence on followers when they have a strong foundation of intrinsic awareness, are self-regulating, can easily connect to others, and exhibit transparency in behaviors (Hernandez et al., 2011; Le Blanc & González-Romá, 2012; Waite et al., 2014). Recently theorists have embarked on a strategy to identify how the most effective individuals develop an authentic leadership posture. As a result of research studies, authenticity has been identified as fundamental to all positive leadership strategies, especially related to authentic leadership (Cianci, Hannah, Roberts, & Tsakumis, 2014).

It has been assessed that authentic leadership develops as a result of early exposure to challenging events in one's career that aids in the need for internal reflection for problem-solving (Waite et al., 2014). These developmental events occur over the course of time to create a foundation of intrinsic values that drive positive decision-making. Additionally, these events promote the growth of ethical standards that support how the individual thinks and behaves, which results in the individual being more capable of seeing things from different perspectives.

By practicing authenticity in leadership, leaders encourage followers to emulate positive attributes in their work behaviors that relate to bringing out the best in their authenticity (Hernandez et al., 2011). In exhibiting self-awareness, authentic leaders are generally introspective and are committed to a strong moral foundation (Hernandez et al., 2011; Waite et al., 2014). Rather than seek to emulate other leaders or comply with the expectations of others, authentic leaders rely on their intrinsic sense of what is right, drawing from their past experiences and desires to have collaborative workplace relationships. This posture is one of the keys to building a foundation of trust in those with whom authentic leaders interact.

Authentic leaders are perceived as trustworthy, highly honorable, and seek to do the right thing for the right reasons. They willingly forego their personal desires and interests for the good of the collective work group (Cianci et al., 2014; Hernandez et al., 2011). They are critically aware of their thoughts and ensure that their behaviors are consistent with what they say and what they promote. They are forthright and will say what they deem is necessary to maintain integrity. Authentic leaders are capable of effectively helping to build and define the organization's identity by helping followers understand who they are in the organization and their importance to the organizational whole (Nichols & Erakovich, 2013).

These leaders know how to connect to others to establish collaborative, trusting relationships and through those established relationships, they know how to achieve results (Waite et al., 2014). This foundation of influence is not always easily identifiable as it is not a concept that is widely talked about or recognized in organizations. The power of influence is generally that illusive "something" that a leader has that prompts team members to respond without dknowing why they are responding. As such, authenticity combined with non-formal social power sources are the foundation upon which positive informal leadership has its greatest influence (Nichols & Erakovich, 2013).

The Informal Leader Connection

Because of the complex nature of the workplace, leadership should be a shared paradigm with the informal leaders being empowered with some level of decision-making authority (Khan & Katzenbach, 2007; Krueger, 2013; Ng'ambi & Bozalek, 2013). When the formal structure cannot always wield the level of influence needed to effect behavior, the informal structure can wield the needed influence to support individuals' behaviors and performance. In most of the organizations, it is difficult to identify the informal authority figure because the strength of the informal leadership structure is defined by how followers feel, what they think, the strength of relationships, and workplace interactions.

Business strategist and authors, Zia Khan and Jon Katzenbach declared that when organizations can integrate the formal and informal structures effectively, they will garner an advantage for enhanced long-term success (Khan & Katzenbach, 2007). Informal leadership research suggests that the informal leader's role should be expanded because today's informal leader is highly knowledgeable with targeted expertise and competencies that could lend itself to helping achieve the organization's vision (Downey et al., 2011; Krueger, 2013; Ng'ambi & Bozalek, 2013; Ross, 2014). Because of the knowledge and expertise of the informal leader in the workplace, these leaders should be more readily acknowledged and garner more respect from senior leaders and those in formal leadership positions. The positive influence of the informal leader has the propensity to lead to progress; the negative influence can result in chaos.

Authentic informal leaders generally exhibit specified intrinsic strengths that enhance how they are perceived by followers and for which informal leaders have consistently scored higher than formal leaders (Crossman & Crossman, 2011; Hernandez et al., 2011; Pielstick, 2000; Waite et al., 2014). These areas include shared vision, communication, relationships, community, and guidance. Shared vision includes the capacity to relay meaning and purpose in a way to incite, inspire, motivate, and unify followers to engage in the vision of the organization. Communication pertains to being able to clarify vision and values through words and actions in such a way that followers understand and to which they connect.

The Follower Philosophy

Although not extensive, a few researchers have endeavored to bring awareness to the role of the follower in promoting successful workplace outcomes (Crossman & Crossman, 2011; DeOrtentiis, Summers, Ammeter, Douglas, & Ferris, 2013; Pielstick, 2000; Sy, 2010). A follower is best defined as an individual in an organization who, united with a team leader, to help a company succeed in achieving goals and objectives. In essence, a follower is any employee who is employed to perform work for the company to produce its products or services. Effective followers are willing to use their acquired competencies and critical thinking skills to work on behalf of the organization and accept responsibility for their role. The ultimate goal of the leadership paradigm is to engage team members to such a degree that team members willingly embrace organizational goals and objectives.

Within the model of self-sacrificial leadership, leaders relinquish their personal desires related to work output, recognition, and power for the benefit of the organization (Arnold & Loughlin, 2010; McKenna & Brown, 2011; Ruggieri & Abbate, 2013). The model purports that by exhibiting self-sacrifice, leaders influence followers to reciprocate sacrifice by exhibiting extra work effort and citizenship behaviors, which then becomes part of the follower's pattern of behavior . In researching the critical role of followers in achieving organizational success, researchers challenged that effective leaders cannot lead without followers who recognized that leaders and followers are mutually responsible for quality workplace relationships and providing high-performance output.

This concept is much aligned with Follettt Parker's concept of the joint control of industry, which supported that the most productive employers engage employees in cooperative efforts for organizational success (Bathurst & Monin, 2010; Follettt Parker, 1918). Follettt Parker advocated integration of non-coercive power-sharing between leaders and followers to promote greater follower engagement and empowerment to achieve organizational goals. She proposed that the workplace complexities of the age mandated leaders and followers work collaboratively to achieve outlined goals and objectives.

The concept of followership focuses on how followers respond to leaders in terms of follower performance, workplace relationships, and a desire to be partners in organizational outcomes (Crossman & Crossman, 2011; DeConinck, 2010; Le Blanc & González-Romá, 2012; Sy, 2010). In the social exchange process within workplace situations, when leaders provide the guidance, direction, and knowledge to the interaction, followers must be receptive enough to embrace the relationship and the responsibility for quality work. When leaders exhibit confidence in follower capabilities and set expectations accordingly, followers are more apt to perform successfully in accordance with expectations.

Leader-Member Exchange

The concept of the leader-member exchange (LMX) has become a topic of broad discussion and targeted interest in leadership research when it comes to the concept of followership (Jha & Jha, 2013; Johnson & Jackson, 2012; Rosen, Harris, & Kacmar, 2011). Most of the management and leadership theories focus on either the leader or the follower as separate targets of study. LMX is unique in that it is among the limited few that incorporates both perspectives and the integration of the two and supports that a leader's interaction is not always equal with each of his or her followers. The basic premise is that leaders generally have different relationships with each team members, whether intentionally or otherwise.

Professor emeritus, Peter Northouse, facilitated extensive research on LMX and proposes a direct correlation between a subordinate's (members) workplace performance based on the relationship with their supervise (leader) (Northouse, 2008). His collective research confirmed that a vertical dyadic relationship does exist. A dyadic relationship is the interaction between two people involved in a social exchange, which can be applied to personal or professional relationships.

The theory posits that leaders develop varying levels of exchanges or relationships with each subordinate over time while relying on formal authority to obtain desired levels of performance from the remaining subordinate population (Jha & Jha, 2013; Johnson & Jackson, 2012; Rosen et al., 2011). It further defines that some relationships are more inclusive and connected to the leader than others and are identified as either in-groups or out-groups. The quality of these two group exchanges has a direct influence on follower attitudes, actions, and behaviors.

The Social Exchange in LMX

Social exchange theory is fundamental to effective dyadic LMX relationships. Social exchange theory is a social psychological concept that explains social interactions as a progressive process of negotiated interactions between targeted parties (Jha & Jha, 2013; Kuvaas, Buch, Dysvik, & Haerem, 2012; Rosen et al., 2011). Within these constructs, individuals who experience or receive positive interactions perceive a sense of indebtedness to the giver of the positive action. When the receiver returns a positive action to the giver, the perception of being in debt to the giver will be reduced within the social exchange. The theory centers around a subordinate's perception of an obligation to respond positively to high-quality workplace exchange relationships.

LMX posits that there are three primary exchange currencies by which the interpersonal exchange in the workplace develops: task behaviors, also known as contribution; loyalty behaviors; and likability or affect (Jha & Jha, 2013; Law, Wang, & Hui, 2010). Task behavior or contribution encompasses a leader's appraisal of the members work output. Loyalty is the leader's perception of the reciprocity within the exchange between the leader and member that promotes trust. Likability or affect refers to the extent that the leader and member enjoy interacting and collaborating with each other.

A fourth currency, respect, was added as subsequent research was conducted on the influence of LMX on employee engagement (Law et al., 2010). The currency of professional respect refers to the extent that the leader and member respect each other's professional expertise and roles. The LMX relationship can be based on any combination of identified currencies, which directly influences the quality of the exchanges and determines whether members are placed in the in-group or out-group.

The Quality of the LMX

Leader-member exchanges are classified as high-quality or low-quality exchange relationships (Jha & Jha, 2013; Law et al., 2010). High-quality LMX relationships are generally characterized by mutual trust, reciprocal respect, and team engagement, whereas low-quality LMX is characterized by constructs being exhibited at lower levels, which negatively impacts employee productivity (Johnson & Jackson, 2012; Kuvaas et al., 2012; Law et al., 2010; Le Blanc & González-Romá, 2012). The prevailing concept is that a reciprocity dynamic is created when a leader contributes positively to the development of a member, thereby laying the foundation for a high-quality exchange. As a result of the high-quality exchange, the member perceives an obligation to the leader and reciprocates by giving equally positive work effort. Reciprocally, as the member's performance increases, the more the leader tends to invest in the member with increased support, resources, and responsibility.

Although a high-quality LMX is associated with improved member performance, there is still some discussion concerning how the exchange and reciprocity process align to create the positive relationship (Johnson & Jackson, 2012; Kuvaas et al., 2012; Law et al., 2010; Le Blanc & González-Romá, 2012). This can be best explained by the group interaction from the leader's perspective base on whether the subordinate is connected to the in-group or out-group. LMX proposes that leaders have bonded relationships with a select group of trusted individuals within their organization, termed in-group members. Those in the leader's in-group or who have a high level of similarity are granted a high level of trust because they are perceived to work harder, possess more loyalty, and are more committed to the leader and the organization. Out-group or less similar members have low-quality LMX or poor relationships with their immediate supervisors and are perceived as individuals who only comply with minimum requirements as outlined in the employment contract and in workplace interactions.

Even the wisest of leaders have to guard against the natural inclination to connect to individuals who are more like them. From an organizational development perspective, it is termed the similar-to-me bias, which basically means as humans we have a tendency to connect better to people who are more like us, that is, look like us, think like us, from similar backgrounds, similar values, etc. Although this is perfectly acceptable in an individual's private life, such preferential treatment can be detrimental in leadership decision-making.

As a result of the preferential treatment, in-group members will likely perform better on the job and put in the extra work to maintain favor (Johnson & Jackson, 2012; Kuvaas et al., 2012; Law et al., 2010; Le Blanc & González-Romá, 2012). They will be perceived by the formal leader as more engaged in their responsibilities and be treated with more favor on the job as a result. This reciprocal engagement scenario is considered high-quality LMXs. These exchanges result in better evaluations, reduced turnover, and overall, more organizational commitment. However, it will lead to feelings of devaluation for out-group members and could potentially lead to disengagement and potential formal complaints. Because they are not a part of the leader's in-group, out-group members might be subjected to more formal channels of supervision and are generally expected to follow formal processes more stringently. These interactions are considered low-quality LMX and can result in a divided work group. The informal leader in such circumstances can serve as a bridge in helping formal leaders understand why the disconnect has occurred.

Informal Leader Identified

Participant in this informal leadership study clearly identified informal leaders in each work group. All agreed that the informal leader wielded some level of influence with 75% of participants stating that the informal leader was highly influential in the team dynamic and 25% supporting that the informal leader was marginally influential. Sixty percent of participants classified the informal leader as a positive influencer and 40% classified the informal leader as a negative influence on the team. Of the 60% of participants who identified a positive informal leader, the majority supported that the informal leader directly influenced team member work behaviors and team interactions.

For those who identified that the informal leader was negative, the majority stated that tried not to allow the negativity of the informal leader to influence their individual work behavior. However, they associated negative words to the informal leader such as insincere, self-centered, self-seeking, aggressive, non-collaborative, sneaky, passive aggressive, confrontational, argumentative, disgruntled, arrogant, manipulative, unsupported, sabotaging, and inconsistent. These behaviors will invariably cause a negative impact on the overall team interactions. Negative informal leaders were described as power brokers who were generally quick to step up and volunteer to get things done. However, it was never for the benefit of the team but generally to get credit and shine.

For those who were deemed to be positive informal leaders, participants used descriptive words such as visionary, go-getter, hardworking, team oriented, honest, solutions driven, collaborative, helpful, respectful, trustworthy, determined, and engaging. Participants supported that these informal leaders wielded great influence on individuals and on the team as a whole. Participants supported that the positive informal leaders were instrumental in bringing teams together and inspiring team member collaborations, even in the midst of conflict. These informal leaders would consistently go above and beyond for the good of the team and did not hesitate to share the spotlight. When they talk, everyone listened. The positive informal leader was perceived to be instrumental in how team member engaged formal leadership authority and promoted a strong foundation for team unity.

4 Team Development Effectiveness

Teams develop in organizations with the expectation that teaming promotes better utilization of individual skill and leverages specialized expertise while minimizing individual work overload (DeChurch & Mesmer-Magnus, 2010; DeOrtentiis et al., 2013). Organizations increasingly rely on teams to accomplish the diverse tasks required for continued operations using the varied base of knowledge existent within the team dynamic (Resick, Dickson, Mitchelson, Allison, & Clark, 2010). According to foundational research by social psychologists, John French and Bertram Raven, both formal and informal leadership considerably influences team interactions and follower behaviors in the team environment (French & Raven, 1959).

Advantages of Teams

In an organizational setting, a work group is simply an assembly of individuals gathered to work to complete a task and share information (DeOrtentiis et al., 2013; Resick et al, 2010). The term "team" can be best defined as a targeted group of individuals with complementary skills, committed to a common objective with defined performance goals for which they are held mutually accountable to achieve an outlined mission. Team members willingly interact interdependently to accomplish a goal or objective with shared or aligned values.

All groups are not teams, but every team begins as a group with a mission (Mahembe & Engelbrecht, 2013). In groups, the focus is on individual performance and achieving individual goals, whereas the focus of teams is on the performance output of the team as a whole. In teams, each member holds themselves and each other accountable for achieving needed outcomes. If one person on a team does not perform proficiently, the entire team suffers, and the team goal will be jeopardized. Table 4.1 outlines the differences between teams and groups (Gilley & Kerno, 2010; Johnson, Hollenbeck, Scott, Barnes, & Jundt, 2013; Stone, 2010).

DOI: 10.4324/9780429319969-5

Table 4.1 Differences in Teams Versus Groups

Teams vs. Groups	
Groups	**Teams**
• Restrictions imposed on individuality; conformity is expected.	• Individuality is strongly encouraged and mutual respect a tenet.
• Thinking outside the box is rarely encouraged or expected.	• Creativity is encouraged and expected as a basis for team collaboration.
• Loyalty is demanded at all costs, or group exclusion is threatened.	• Dissenting ideas and concepts are urged as a basis for team success.
• Individuals are me-focused, interested in how things can best to benefit them.	• Individuals are team-focused, interested in how team goals can be accomplished.
• Communication is streamlined for quick decision-making.	• Open communication advocated to prompt divergent views.
• Conflict is avoided; compliance expected.	• Conflicts are embraced as opportunities to grow; resolution a prime goal.

Because individual brings varied perspectives, experiences, and knowledge to team interactions, teams are expected to make higher quality decisions to successfully achieve set goals (Johnson et al., 2013). For teams to be maximally effective, it is important for team members to know why they exist and for all members to be committed to achieving team goals to maximize effectiveness.

Team Effectiveness – Kaizen Model

Research findings support that team effectiveness and performance proficiency are connected to team composition and positive team interactions (Resick et al., 2010). Various studies have sought to identify the sources of team cohesion and team turmoil in hopes of providing insight into building a strong team foundation (Mahembe & Engelbrecht, 2013; Resick et al., 2010; Rosh, Offermann, & Van Diest, 2012). Understanding the source of these dynamics and the principles of strategic team development will enhance a leader's capacity to promote effective team building and team productivity.

Research suggested that strategic team development must incorporate the concept of lean thinking to maximize continuous process improvements and minimize waste in resources and productivity (Johnson et al., 2013; Rolfsen & Johansen, 2014; Stone, 2010). The lean team concept is known as kaizen teams and is more commonly referred to as self-managed, self-directed, or self-regulating teams. Modern references to high-performing teams refer to the kaizen or self-managed team concept. These teams are composed of members who have high levels of control over their task accomplishment, decision-making, and work methodologies.

Kaizen teams differ from ordinary teams primarily based on the level of autonomy granted to team members and are deemed to have greater sustainability in organizational operations (Rolfsen & Johansen, 2014; Johnson et al., 2013; Stone, 2010). They are perceived to be better positioned as tactical performers to identify problems, determine core causes, and understand the impact on the organization. These teams are better equipped to rapidly change task strategy to accommodate organizational changes or to rectify performance deficiencies. As a result, these teams are given more authority and freedom in how members accomplish team tasks to ensure operational success.

Despite the popularity of the concept, kaizen or self-managed teams have been criticized by some organizational researchers for having too much autonomy (Gilley & Kerno, 2010; Johnson et al., 2013; Rolfsen & Johansen, 2014). The primary concerns are that these team members may not always have all critical information to make the best judgment call to make the best decision. Furthermore, these teams may make the best decision for the team's interest but may not be able to or willing to make the best decision in the organization's best interest. Despite these concerns, the kaizen concept of high-performing teams continues to be one of the most discussed leadership topics in organizational operations, especially related to effective responses to organizational change. It is important for leader to understand how team effectiveness develops and utilize proven strategies to make it happen.

Tuckman's Team Development Model

Organizational leaders now realize that the use of effective teams provides better business results than depending on the talent of a single individual. It is, therefore, important that leaders understand the stages of team development and how groups develop to ensure team effectiveness. Group development models were conceptualized to explain how groups transition from a group of individuals with varying drivers to a productive team oriented towards a productive unit. In an organizational setting, group development falls into three categories: linear progressive models, cyclical models, and nonsequential models (Gilley & Kerno, 2010; Morita & Burns, 2014).

The linear progressive model holds that groups develop in a linear direction, progressively maturing over time. The first critical effort and best known referenced linear progressive model is Tuckman and Jensen's Five-Stage Model (Gilley & Kerno, 2010; Hare, 2010; Morita & Burns, 2014).

The model described five linear stages through which groups progress in the development into a productive team. The stages include forming, storming, norming, performing, and adjourning (in some cases termed transforming).

Forming involves the process that initially brings individuals together to achieve a common goal (Gilley & Kerno, 2010; Morita & Burns, 2014). In this stage, individuals transition from being separate entities to members of a group on a mission for a targeted purpose. Individuals are typically not only excited about the project but also anxious about understanding the tasks that must be accomplished and how progress will be made. Initial processes include defining goals and strategizing how to ensure goal success. Often during this stage, group members will begin to show signs of impatience, irritation, and some anxiety.

Storming is the process members go through when the feelings of impatience, irritation, and anxiety manifest into disagreements (Gilley & Kerno, 2010; Morita & Burns, 2014). These levels of discord are healthy expectations of development as individuals begin the process of understanding roles, viewpoints, limitations, and possible directions to achieve best outcomes. This stage is characterized by tension and arguments among individuals as they begin to process the realities of what the project will entail. Individuals assess each other's character, behaviors, and mindsets, while reconciling how to best integrate the differences to move forward. This is one of the most difficult stages of team development as individuals begin to try to assess where they fit in the group and conflicts arise.

Conflict will generally be based on one of the four root causes: personality-based, role-based, leader-based, or work-style conflict (Buljac, Van Woerkom, Van Wijngaarden, & Ananthaswamy, 2013). Personality-based conflict, the most common source of discord, occurs when vastly different personalities clash. Leader-based conflicts arise when the designated formal leader's leadership style is not aligned with the way group members expectations. Role-based conflict occurs when individuals in the group compete for informal roles in the group dynamic. Work-style conflict occurs when group members begin to realize the differences in how each member works and accomplishes work tasks.

Many groups will get stuck in the phase and see very little progress towards goal achievement (Buljac et al., 2013). If group members are unable to process through this stage, team effectiveness will be minimized, and potentially team goals will fail. However, to maximize effectiveness, group members must process through the discord to bond as a team. Group members will generally go to the individual who is easy to talk to, or who can help clarify differences and promote resolution. These various conflict scenarios provide ample opportunities for a strong informal leader to position as the "go to" resource to promote team cohesion and growth.

During *Norming*, group member will begin to see themselves as team members and begin to establish a foundation of collaboration and trust (Gilley & Kerno, 2010; Morita & Burns, 2014). During this stage, the team culture is established as team members develop a sense of cohesion, establish ground rules, and agree on team operations. The turmoil will begin to diminish, and team members begin to work productively, forging productive alliances and relationships among team members. Team members begin to accept each other's strengths and weaknesses as well as establish a foundation of respect in embracing team roles. The team can generally see that they are making progress towards the goal. During this stage, the formal and informal leader will have also worked out a collaborative foundation of co-existence.

Performing is the stage in which leaders want to see most team reach (Gilley & Kerno, 2010; Morita & Burns, 2014). In this stage, team members are collectively facilitating assigned tasks and responsibilities for which the team was established. Fully functioning as a team, team members are working together effectively, making decisions, implementing them, and solving problems. They are actively progressing towards achieving team objectives and operating as one unit. Conflict may still arise, but because team members have grown to know and respect each other, they have the ability to work through conflicts and avoid stalemates. This is when the team begins to exhibit kaizen attributes to high performance.

The last stage of the team development model involves one of two paths to which the team can progress, *Adjourning or Transforming* (Gilley & Kerno, 2010; Morita & Burns, 2014). If the team was brought together for a specified project or period, when the tasks are accomplished, the team will cease to exist or adjourn, ending the temporary team assignment. Most teams, however, are not established for such brief periods of time. Thus, if the team was established as a continual component in the organizational operations, the team dynamic will change in time or go through levels of transformation.

The most common change or transformation will involve one team member leaving or a new team member joining the team (Gilley & Kerno, 2010; Morita & Burns, 2014). Transforming in the team development model has only been recognized within the last ten years. It acknowledges that when a member leaves or another joins, the team goes through many of the previously identified four stages as the new member is acclimated into the team. Likewise, if a team member leaves and the responsibilities of the exiting team members are distributed among the remaining members, the team may revert to storming before norming or performing. Throughout Tuckman and Jensen's Five-Stage Model, the formal and informal leadership roles are instrumental in helping the team progress from through each stage in order to achieve established goals.

Wheelan's Integrated Model

A second foundational team development model was conceived by psychology professor, Susan Wheelan. Wheelan's Integrated Model of Group Development builds upon Tuckman's research findings (Bonebright, 2010; Hare, 2010). The model is premised on the assumption that groups develop into productive teams over the course of working together and achieves maturity through daily interactions and collaboration. Although linear in a sense, the difference between Tuckman and Wheelan's theory is Wheelan concept of team maturity. She assessed that groups achieve maturity by their continual interaction and enhanced by verbal dialogue.

This four-stage model is premised on the assumption that groups develop into productive teams over the course of time by working through turmoil and strife to achieve maturity (Bonebright, 2010; Hare, 2010). The early stages are benchmarked on getting to know each other as team members through verbal interactions, processing through dependency to trust. As collaboration and interaction increases in the latter or more mature stages, team member begins to do the work to produce the desire outcomes. The stages include dependency and inclusion, counter-dependency and fight, trust and structure, and work and productivity.

Stage 1 is *dependency and inclusion*. This is the phase of team development when the group initially comes together (Bonebright, 2010; Hare, 2010). It has also been referred to as the childhood phase of team development when individuals in the group have a strong interdependence upon each other. Group members rely on the group leader to provide direction and oversight in order to begin to move towards meeting established goals. Members will also be more prone to lean on individuals in the group who tend to have strong personalities or perceived high knowledge in the areas of focus. As a result, informal leaders have a tendency to position to exert authority in the group.

Stage 2, *counter-dependency and fight*, is the stage in which team members begin to have more confidence in their roles on the team and begin to have less dependency on the team leader (Bonebright, 2010; Hare, 2010). Conflict begins to arise as team members feel more comfortable standing as independent thinkers, speaking up when they disagree, and even challenge the formal leader if they have different perspectives related to team operations. Conflict is not only a great possibility in team interaction but also an inevitable component of team development. As they process through this stage, team members begin to understand each member's strengths, weaknesses, and personalities, and bonds of trust or distrust will begin to emerge.

Stage 3 is termed the *trust and structure* phase. By this stage, team members have worked through disagreement and divergent perspectives characterized by the second stage and are more accepting of their individual differences (Bonebright, 2010; Hare, 2010). Team roles have been identified, communication is more open, and team members are purposefully working collaboratively to accomplish outlined goals. As team members worked through conflicts and differences, trust, commitment, and cooperative attitudes increased. This stage is also characterized by more willingness to negotiate with each other concerning roles, processes, and procedures. Team members are also focused on diligently working to establish positive working relationships with each other in an effort to ensure team continuity. During this stage, informal leaders will have an opportunity to position with more authority related to helping to mediate conflict scenarios and promote the formal leader's position of trust in the team.

During stage 4, **work and productivity**, team members are now more cohesive, productive, and effective in accomplishing team goals (Bonebright, 2010; Hare, 2010). This is considered the maturity phase as this is the stage of team development in which trust has been established among team members and the team structure is solidified. This is the stage of targeted productivity as team members spend less time on developing as a team and focus their energy on accomplishing the team's purpose. By this stage of development, to be maximally effective, the formal and informal leader will have established a collaborative relationship to ensure team success.

Nonsequential Team Development Models

The nonsequential models support that the pattern of team development depends largely on environmental factors such as time constraints and task goals (Carillo & Okoli, 2011; Hare, 2010). The tasks to be accomplished and set deadlines are deemed to have more influence on the group development than the interpersonal relationships of the group membership. In this team development paradigm, group members focus strongly on the timeline and the team goal. As a result, those components lead to enhanced performance to achieve set goals on the timeline set. McGrath's Time, Interaction, and Performance theory (TIP) is an example of the nonsequential model of group development.

Founded by social psychologist, Joseph McGrath, the TIP theory proposed that different groups can move through different development paths dependent upon what is needed at a specified time to complete an outlined task or function (Beranek & Clairborne, 2012; Carillo & Okoli, 2011). In the TIP model, not every team followed the same developmental path. Thus, different teams with the same expected outcome could follow a different path. Of the four modes, McGrath proposed that only mode one (inception) and mode four (execution) are required as a beginning and a completion of task outcomes. However, mode two (technical problem-solving) and mode three (conflict resolution) are modes that may or may not be a part of the team's development dependent upon the team's mission.

The cyclical approach to understanding team development proclaims that groups develop through stages but may continually revisit prior stages during the developmental process (Morita & Burns, 2014). They support that teams all deal with similar issues; however, at different times they must deal with unexpected changes to include environmental changes, changes in group membership, and changes in assigned tasks. The cyclical model holds that groups mature in shorter developmental cycles and will modify their approach and strategy to problem-solving based on its prior experience in resolving the same or similar issues. This model mandates flexibility as the group matures into its team dynamic.

Informal Leadership Influence on Team Development

A strong leadership presence in the development of a team can promote the team-building process or undermine a formal leader's effort in the process (Rolfsen & Johansen, 2014). Study participant responses strongly support the influence an informal leader wields in the effectiveness of team development. Whether that individual who is identified as the informal leader is positive or negative has a direct impact on how the team bonds and impacts individual engagement.

The research results supported that the areas in which informal leaders tend to be most influential included information sharing, team productivity, and team member interactions. These leaders were described as social, influential, with the capacity to engage. As a result, even if negative, the informal leader was deemed as someone who influenced the team. When negative, it was deemed that their attitude could dismantle the team by causing chaos or cause the team to get stuck in storming.

Team Cognition and Mental Modeling

Due to the expansive growth of the team concept in the workplace, leaders are increasingly concerned with assuring teams are positioned for effective decision-making (DeChurch & Mesmer-Magnus, 2010; DeOrtentiis et al., 2013; Nasomboon, 2014). Team decision-making behaviors are contingent on members reaching a common foundation of understanding and appreciation for other team member's contributions. Effective decision-making in the team environment mandates team members integrate individual viewpoints to enhance perceptions of equity, encourage greater decision-making engagement, and promote commitment to implement decisions.

Effective teams must be able to maximize the knowledge and expertise of team members without over tasking individuals (Cooke, Gorman, Myers, & Duran, 2013; DeOrtentiis et al., 2013). To facilitate the strategy, teams must develop team cognition structures to enhance knowledge sharing and decision-making. Team cognition represents the way team members understand, process, and use available knowledge and information to accomplish tasks within the team paradigm (Cooke et al., 2013; Resick et al., 2010). This concept has been deemed the key to predicting the effectiveness of team interactions. Although strategies to measure team cognition are still not well-defined, the concept suggests that it is an important element in helping team members collectively focus on accomplishing the goal as a single unit rather than focusing on individual competitiveness. Thus, it is a critical component on building the foundation to a high-performing collaborative team.

Team cognition is important to teaming because it encourages team members to focus on utilizing their individual knowledge with that of their teammates to ensure team goals are accomplished (Cooke et al., 2013; Resick et al., 2010). In the formal leader survey, the participating engaged leaders were asked what was their strategies in building high-performing teams. Although the term team cognition was never used, the feedback suggested that this concept was essential to assuring a strong foundation for team members to work as a cohesive unit to achieve team goals. The leaders found it important to assess team members' individual strengths and weaknesses, and then allow each team member to serve in their areas of strength. They let team members know that their team contributions are valued and essential to the team operating as a unified body.

To assimilate the diversity of skill and expertise on a team, team members must develop a foundation to willingly share and appreciate the skill, knowledge, and abilities each member brings to the team Lai, Lam & Lam (2013. This collective appreciation of shared knowledge is termed the team's cognitive structures and is purported to enhance a team's capacity to process information, adapt to change, respond to team member needs, and make effective decisions based on what is best for the team rather than for individual gain (Cooke et al., 2013;). Team cognition motivates group members to engage in collaborative teamwork, predict work outcomes, adapt to the circumstances, and focus on maximizing team effectiveness (Kozlowski & Chao, 2012; Resick et al., 2010). If team cognition is absent or ineffective, team members will limit knowledge sharing and team member interactions, resulting in ineptness in collaborating, problem-solving, or decision-making.

Effective teams must be able to maximize the knowledge and expertise of team members to develop team cognition structures to enhance knowledge sharing and decision-making (Cooke et al., 2013; Gijselaers, Woltjer, Segers, van den Bossche, & Kirschner, 2011). This strengthens the team's identity, which helps them bond as a team in achieving goals (Ruggieri & Abbate, 2013). Within the purview of team cognition, researchers have determined that the best strategy to enhance team cognition and strengthen team identity is through understanding the team member's mental models.

Mental Models and Team Collaboration

Mental models are the cognitive processes that help humans interpret various constructs to understand the world and their environment (DeChurch & Mesmer-Magnus, 2010: Resick et al., 2010). In the workplace, mental modeling in teams is foundational to how team members assess the teams value to the organization, how they meld as a unit, and how much they want to interact and collaborate. It allows teams to understand how they organize and share information and knowledge within the team environment, especially as it relates to team cohesiveness, coordinating team tasks, responding to changing demands, and achieving team success. Modeling also helps teams to align collaborative actions based on a clear understanding of team member roles, strengths, weaknesses, and behaviors.

When the mental models of team members are positively aligned, team members collectively evaluate proposed change actions and integrate their behaviors to act based on the perceptions of the collective whole (DeChurch & Mesmer-Magnus, 2010; Resick et al., 2010). When mental models are strong, individual team members can predict how co-team members will respond to the unexpected, accurately assess how varying circumstances will impact team interactions, and quickly align individual behaviors to what is needed to achieve resolutions to potential team disconnects.

As teams with strong mental models are more interactive and committed to task or goal achievement, they are more successful in accomplishing their long-term goals, are more consistent in performance, and have more positive perceptions of team sustainability (DeChurch & Mesmer-Magnus, 2010; Mahembe & Engelbrecht, 2013; Resick et al., 2010). The greater the separation in team members' mental models, the less team members are likely to be supportive of each, which directly undermines not only the team's foundation of collaboration but also the team's capacity to bond cohesively.

Mental Models and Team Cohesiveness

A cohesive team is considered a team composite in which team members have a clear agreed upon charter, purpose, or common goal wherein each member is willing to work to achieve set goals (Kozlowski & Chao, 2012; Morita & Burns, 2014; Resick et al., 2010). These teams are self-monitoring, empowered to make decisions and solve problems, and have firmly established team norms to assure effective team functioning. Team members are accepting of other's in the group, avoid judging others, and show respect for the thoughts and feelings of all members. Differences of opinion are encouraged and freely expressed (Kozlowski & Chao, 2012; Morita & Burns, 2014). As a result, the team does not demand conformity that inhibits freedom of expression or open brainstorming.

Members in cohesive teams do not avoid conflict, but they embrace variances and actively focus on addressing conflict directly to seek resolution to enhance team effectiveness (Gijselaers et al., 2011; Kozlowski & Chao, 2012; Morita & Burns, 2014; Resick et al., 2010). Team members are interdependent, as they realize they need each other in order to achieve success. Members appreciate each other's knowledge, skills, experiences, and differences. Competition is minimized among members, but focus is placed on valuing and promoting team member engagement and achievements. The team encourages risk taking and creativity in pursuing the goals. Mistakes are treated as tools of learning rather than reasons for punishment.

Strongly cohesive teams are open and responsive to the changing needs of its members and cognizant of the influence of the external environment on the team (Kozlowski & Chao, 2012; Morita & Burns, 2014; Resick et al., 2010). Team members are committed to periodically evaluating team performance in an objective and non-judgmental way and ensure individual team member performance is aligned to team expectations. They hold each other accountable and believe that working together is more synergistic than working alone. Empowering leaders must seek to magnify the aforementioned traits to inspire team members to engage in behaviors that promote team and organizational unity.

5 Organizational Citizenship Behavior

Business research supports that for organizations to achieve long-term success, three employee behaviors are required (Bhuvanaiah & Raya, 2014). Firstly, organizations must be able to persuade external talent to join the organization. Secondly, once the talent is in the organization, they must be motivated to consistently perform assigned tasks and remain with the organization long term. Finally, employees should be engaged to connect with the organizational vision and willingly above and beyond normal expectations when needed. Positive, constructive employee behaviors that go above and beyond normal expectations towards achieving organizational goals have been termed organizational citizenship behaviors (OCBs) (Beheshtifar & Hesani, 2013).

Since its emergence in organizational development research, OCB has developed into a significant field of study. As the traditional hierarchical work structures are being replaced by more autonomous team-based constructs, more study is focused on the importance of OCB on workplace success on the micro and macro level of operations. On the micro level, study is focused on individual employee's performance and role in the organization. On the macro level, research is focused on understanding how team member interactions influence team success and change in the organization.

The OCB concept has been deemed the cornerstone of teamwork in the model called team organizational citizenship behavior (Jiao, Richards, & Zhang, 2011; Qamar, 2012). This construct has been proven to have a strong impact on how team members function in the workplace. However, it is a concept that is rarely discussed in an organizational development context and, from this research perspective, is neither understood nor considered by organizational leadership. In a general context, the concept of citizenship in the workplace encompasses positive, supportive behaviors that are not among core performance expectations but still contribute to organizational effectiveness. Citizenship is the foundation of OCB, focusing on

DOI: 10.4324/9780429319969-6

what individuals intrinsically bring to the work environment that have a wholistic influence on teams and the organization (Organ, 1988; Podsakoff, MacKenzie, Paine, & Bachrach, 2000).

The OCB Concept

In researching the drivers of worker motivation, a clear distinction was made between employees performing assigned job-oriented tasks (*in-role behaviors*) and those engaging in voluntary collaborative or helping behaviors (*extra-role behaviors*) (Belogolovsky & Somech, 2010; Harun, Soran, & Caymaz, 2014; Salavati, Ahmadi, Sheikhesmaeili, & Mirzaei, 2011). Extra-role behaviors are assessed as critical to organizational proficiency and the purview under which OCBs are included. Extra-role behaviors are not defined in a job description but are embraced as a normal aspect of performance based on a desire to see the organization succeed. Although not mandatory, these behaviors are work-related tasks that employees engage in on a voluntary, intentional basis. Fully engaged employees are motivated to greater extra-role behaviors, whereas the disgruntled employee will be prone to less extra role or citizenship behaviors, as well as greater propensity to reject organizational change.

Before one can fully understand how OCB influences team effectiveness, it is important to understand the concept of OCB in the workplace on an individual level (Harun et al., 2014; Jiao et al., 2011; Salavati et al., 2011). The most influential base of research on the concept was conducted by industrial psychology researcher, Dennis Organ (Organ, 1988). Organ's theory of OCB has been the most widely studied and accepted as a psychological reflection of how employees perceive and connect to the work environment.

Discretionary helping behaviors as referenced in Organ's research are those that are not a part of the employee's formal job expectations or terms of employment (Belogolovsky & Somech, 2010; Organ, 1988). When employees engage in citizenship behaviors, the organization perceives great benefits. The presence of OCBs has been described as the good soldier syndrome or pro-social behaviors because they include behaviors that go above what is required by job descriptions (Organ, 1988; Harun et al., 2014; Qamar, 2012; Salavati et al., 2011). Empirical evidence supports that the presence of OCBs enhances the organization by increasing productivity, improving collaborations, decreasing turnover, and reducing conflict (Beheshtifar & Hesani, 2013; Harun et al., 2014; Salavati et al., 2011). As these behaviors are not mandatory, employees will not be subject to formal channels of discipline for failure to exhibit.

Five-Dimensional OCB Model

OCBs include a five-dimensional model inclusive of altruism, courtesy, conscientiousness, sportsmanship, and civic virtue (Organ, 1988; Qamar, 2012; Rego et al., 2010; Salavati et al., 2011). *Altruism* is best defined as the selfless concern for others; helping out of a genuine desire to help and be of service, not out of a sense of obligation and without expectation of return. It involves looking out for the well-being of others. In the workplace, altruism involves providing assistance in a collaborative manner on issues not related to the job description as needed in the work group related to any problems, issues, or concerns.

Courtesy is the display of polite behavior marked by respect for others or showing appropriate social etiquettes (Organ, 1988; Qamar, 2012; Rego et al., 2010; Salavati et al., 2011). It is posturing to share available resources willingly and actively seeking to avoid hurting others, taking advantage of others, or creating problems. In the workplace, these behaviors involve employees exhibiting sincere consideration for others. Examples of this dimension include assisting a coworker complete a project in a timely manner, making a consistent effort to let coworkers know how much they are appreciated as a team member, or simply saying please and thank you as a behavioral norm.

Conscientiousness is defined as an individual's propensity to be trustworthy, reliable, diligent, goal-focused, and dedicated to adhering to the rules (Organ, 1988; Qamar, 2012; Rego et al., 2010; Salavati et al., 2011). A conscientious person is good at regulating their actions and controlling impulses. In the workplace, a conscientious individual is committed to doing a good job regardless of personal gain and consistently perform tasks beyond the minimum requirements or expectations. Examples of conscientious behavior include targeting focused attention on assuring success in a targeted goal or investing extra energy in ensuring a task is as perfectly achieved as possible.

Sportsmanship is defined as exhibiting just and generous behavior of others, treating others fairly and equitably, and tolerating difficulties or inconveniences without protest (Organ, 1988; Qamar, 2012; Rego et al., 2010; Salavati et al., 2011). This OCB dimension encompasses not being offended when others disagree, refusing to take rejection personally, and a willingness to make personal sacrifices for the good of the whole. In the workplace, it entails demonstrating a positive attitude about those with whom one works and the organization, as well as resisting the urge to complain or focus on the negative. Examples of sportsmanship include accepting undesired tasks with a positive attitude and not complaining about tough work assignments.

Civic virtue is the dedicated commitment of a citizen to focus on the common welfare of the community even at the cost of one's individual interests (Organ, 1988; Qamar, 2012; Rego et al., 2010; Salavati et al., 2011). In the workplace, it involves being an advocate for the organization and being proacting in engaging to take the organization to the next level. This OCB dimension is exemplified by behaviors indicative of an employee's intense concerns and fervent interest in the life of the organization. Civic virtue differs from other OCBs in that the behavior is focused on the macro-level interest in the organization as a whole, rather than individual team interactions.

Research supports that as single constructs, these five traits will generally make no notable difference on macro-level organizational operations (Podsakoff et al., 2000; Rego et al., 2010). Original study of the concept focused on the micro level or individual impact of these constructs because the behaviors begin with individual team members. However, research consistently supports that when these dimensions are exhibited as cumulative and consistent patterns of behavior by team members, employee workplace satisfaction (micro level) and team productivity (macro level) are enhanced, and organizational proficiency and operational effectiveness are improved.

The Influence of OCB

Most OCB research is directly linked to OCB at the individual level (OCBI) (Lai, Lam, & Lam, 2013; Lin & Peng, 2010; Yu-Chen, 2014). However, with the preponderance of change in the workplace and a desire for more organizational effectiveness, more studies are now focused on the influence of OCB on the team dynamic in organizations (OCBO). OCBI benefits include an open willingness to help coworkers, consistency in attendance, resiliencies in response to uncertainty, and an inherent desire to exceed base expectations. Employees who exhibited OCBI were less likely to consider leaving the organization, which enhanced retention and productivity (Podsakoff et al., 2000; Salavati et al., 2011).

Benefits of OCBO, also called Group OCB, include increased pro-social team member interactions, ease of compliance to organization guidelines, open knowledge sharing, and adaptability to change or uncertainty (Lin & Peng, 2010; Salavati et al., 2011; Yu-Chen, 2014). Organ's research suggests that individuals who exhibit high OCBI have the potential of improving the productivity of any team on which the individual performs. Conversely, low OCBI can result in individuals who have little desire to be a part of a team or fully invest in organizational goals. Research suggests that an employee's willingness to engage in pro-social behaviors is aligned with how they perceived organizational justice.

Organizational Justice and OCB

The limited research conducted on OCBs in the team environment supported that how employees feel about their leader has a direct influence on individual and team OCB (Choi & Sy, 2010; Lai et al., 2013; Yu-Chen, 2014). The concept of organizational justice is foundational to the perceptions an employee has of the leader and the organization as a whole (Schilpzand, Martins, Kirkman, Lowe, & Chen, 2013). These perceptions are determinants of what drives the employee's decision to go that extra mile to ensure success of change initiatives and proactively promote of change goals.

Organizational justice refers to an employee's perception of fairness in the organization related to all aspects of workplace behavior (Titrek, Polatcan, Zafer Gunes, & Sezen, 2014). The concept maintains that an employee's assessment of their organization's behaviors, decisions, and actions has a direct influence on the employee's own attitudes and behaviors at work. Research suggests that employees compare what they perceive as benefits or gains in working in the organization and in their position with what others in similar organizations with similar positions are doing. The comparisons include everything from leadership quality, supervisory treatment, access to training, gender equality, pay, and incentives.

The assessment of the comparison will determine the employee's judgment of their organization's behavior and how the behavior influences employees' attitudes and performance (Schilpzand et al., 2013; Titrek et al., 2014). When employees assess that they are being treated fairly and equitably as compared to the object of their comparison, they will have positive attitudes towards their leader and organization. In accordance with social exchange theory, the positive attitudes will promote and result in pro-social workplace behaviors in return (DeConinck, 2010; Schilpzand et al., 2013). In essence, perceived organizational justice inspires workplace OCB whereby employees reciprocate citizenship behaviors for fair treatment (Batool, 2013).

Employee perceptions of organizational justice can be classified by four justice categories: distributive, procedural, interpersonal, and informational (DeConinck, 2010; Yilmaz & Altinkurt, 2012). *Distributive justice* reflects perceptions regarding fairness of outcomes within the organization. It is defined as the assessment of an employee's perceptions in how allowances and compensations are shared or distributed across various group members in the organization. Allowances involve non-compensatory activities, such as time off and choice assignments. Compensations can take any forms, including salaries, bonuses, allowances, incentives, and promotional opportunities.

This category entails three potential levels of comparison: individual equity, what they bring to the table; comparative equity, how they measure up to others in the organization; and external equity, comparison to like situated external organizations, external equity (DeConinck, 2010; Yilmaz & Altinkurt, 2012). External equity is less influential than individual or comparative equity. Upon assessment, if the employee's experiences or expectations fall short, distributive justice will be judged to be absent in the organization.

Procedural justice is focused on how decisions are made, and how policies are established and applied in the organization (DeConinck, 2010; Yilmaz & Altinkurt, 2012). Procedural justice is perceived to be present when employees believe that the important process decisions and outcomes are fair and just for all and not advantageous for a select few. Key elements of procedural justice concern the transparency with which important decisions are made, resources are allocated, and conflict is resolved. Two critical areas of this justice category involve the administration of justice and retributive justice. Administration of justice is the perception of how employees feel the organization manages processes related to managing daily work, implementing policies, and allocating resources. Retributive justice is the assessment of how fairly conflict and disputes are resolved, wrongdoing is dealt with, and infractions punished.

Employees must perceive that decisions are being made without prejudice or partiality (DeConinck, 2010; Yilmaz & Altinkurt, 2012). This second form of organization justice has a direct impact on how employees respond to change initiatives and how readily they engage to help ensure success. If procedural justice is deemed to be low or absent, employees will not trust that processes and procedures related to the change will be advantageous to their time, commitment, or efforts. As a result, pro-change behavior will be minimized and potential for change resistance increased.

Interpersonal justice is best defined as the degree to which employees feel that decisions made reflect that they are treated with dignity and respect (DeConinck, 2010; Yilmaz & Altinkurt, 2012). It reflects perceptions of how employees interact, relate to, and treat each other at work to include manager-subordinate and coworker interactions. When employees feel a high level of respect is exhibited, they will regard the organization as fair and a safe place to work. If interpersonal interactions are perceived as fair, employees tend to respond to change with optimism and engagement. Thus, during organizational change, this justice concept significantly influences to what degree employees commit to change interventions.

If an employee perceives that interpersonal injustice exists, feelings of resentment, anger, and bitterness against leaders and the organization will develop, which will result in counter-productive work behaviors (CWBs) and reduce organizational effectiveness (DeConinck, 2010; Yilmaz & Altinkurt, 2012). CWBs are behaviors that employees voluntarily or intentionally engage in that result in harm to organizations.

Informational justice is defined as employee perceptions as to whether timely and quality information is shared with employees during and after process decisions are made and action executed (DeConinck, 2010; Yilmaz & Altinkurt, 2012). In essence, it is how effectively information and knowledge are shared between leadership and employees in the organization. Within this concept, perceptions are shaped through leadership explanations, which are the basic processes related to information flow between managers and subordinates. Leadership explanations are expected to clearly inform employees as to why certain processes and procedures were chosen and the impact on all stakeholders. When leadership explanations are clear and perceived as fair to all organizational constituents, the organization is perceived to be just.

When it comes to change initiatives in the organization, this level of organizational justice is contingent upon information from social accounts (DeConinck, 2010; Yilmaz & Altinkurt, 2012). Social accounts are leadership explanations given to justify leadership decisions and actions related to change initiatives and interventions. Research suggests that how leadership explanations and social account information is shared has direct influence on employee responses to change initiatives. If information justice is perceived favorably, employee cooperation and engagement are high. If there are perceptions of information injustice, employees may be prone to withdrawal, disconnection, and resistance related to change initiatives.

When employee perceptions of organizational justice are strong, there are much higher probabilities of positive employee reactions to change and pro-change behaviors (DeConinck, 2010; Yilmaz & Altinkurt, 2012). Research supports that when the four categories of organizational justice are perceived as high, OCB in the workplace is stronger. However, the effect of each justice category on pro-change behavior will be dependent upon the degree to which employees identify with their organization. Fair procedures (procedural justice) and the fair provision or allocation of resources (distributive justice) have been found to influence how employee's feel about their value to the organization and thus effect an employee's capacity to identify with their organization.

Organizational Identity and OCB

Merriam-Webster defines identity as the unconscious process in which an individual models the thoughts, feelings, and actions of an identified object. It is the process by which individuals connect in a social sense and make sense of their world and thoughts in an effort to aid in decision-making. The concept of identification in the organizational process is the degree with which the organization and its constituents have similar values, objectives, and desires. The concept refers to the propensity of an employee to identify with the organization and its leadership (Lin, 2004; Ravasi & Phillips, 2011). In essence, Organizational Identity nswers the following questions: who are we, what do we do, and why are we here?

Organizational identity is an employee's internal view of the organization and how the employee frames their concept of their connection to the organization (Lin, 2004; Lin & Peng, 2010). The framework of the employee's perception involves three criteria to enhance an employee's perception of organizational identity: centrality, distinctiveness, and durability (Lin, 2004; Ravasi & Phillips, 2011). Centrality defines what is important and essential to the organization existence, to include the organization's central strengths and weaknesses. Distinctiveness refers to the organization's ability to distinguish itself from other organizations and define what makes it unique. Durability refers to the organization's capacity to endure and maintain its identity, even in the midst of change. When these three tenants are present, it suggests the organization has a strong identity and it helps employees understand how they identify with the organization.

The concept of organizational identification is the degree to which employees feel a sense of unity with the organization and to which they perceive a psychological connection to the organization and its purpose (Lin, 2004; Ravasi & Phillips, 2011). As employees realize they share the values of the organization, they will begin to commit to working more diligently to achieve organizational goals. They will also work more collaboratively with other individuals, working as a unified team on behalf of the organization rather than disconnected units. The higher the level of organizational identification, the more employees will invest in dedicating themselves to help the organization succeed. An employee's connection to organizational identification is directly correlated to the level of an employee's organizational trust (Nichols & Erakovich, 2013; Waite et al., 2014).

The Element of Organizational Trust

Statistics support a growing concern for the level of distrust in organizational leadership (Cho & Park, 2011;. This is significant as research strongly supports that inter-organizational trust is critical to the long-term stability of the organization and the well-being of its stakeholders (Cho & Park, 2011;). When faced with the uncertainty in the workplace, especially related to workplace change, research suggests that employee reactions will be heavily driven by employee perceptions of fairness (organizational justice) and commitment (organizational identification). The most critical aspect of an employee's assessment of organizational justice and identification is trust.

The definition of trust is rooted in employee's belief that the organization will always act in their best interest (; Levine, 2010; Yilmaz & Altinkurt, 2012). This belief encompasses vulnerability and the risk of one's vulnerability being violated. From an organizational context, trustworthiness is the assessment of the level of confidence an employee has in a leader honoring the responsibilities inherent within the organizational social contract.

Organizational trustworthiness encompasses leadership behaviors that reinforce employees' perceptions that the organization will act in the best interest of its employees without doubt, hesitation, or fear Yilmaz & Altinkurt, 2012). When trust is high in the organizational paradigm, employees are less prone to react negatively to uncertainties and more likely to exhibit pro-social behaviors. Organizational trust is instrumental in how employees engage leadership, keep their commitments, communicate honestly, and avoid taking advantage of the organization or its constituents.

The concept of trust has been directly linked to the overall job satisfaction and social exchanges, which is foundational to employee attitudes and behaviors as well as their perceptions of fairness (DeConinck, 2010; Yilmaz & Altinkurt, 2012). Trust is enhanced and increased when employees believe the organization has treated them fairly in the allocation of resources (distributive justice). It is additionally heightened when employees feel they have a participative voice in how they are evaluated in performance measures (procedural justice). It is further magnified when employees perceive that their leaders are committed to treating them with consistency and equity (interpersonal justice).

Research supports a strong correlation between organizational justice and pro-change behaviors as it connects to organizational identification (Batool, 2013; Titrek et al., 2014; Yilmaz & Altinkurt, 2012). As a result, the higher the perceived levels of organizational justice and organizational identification, the more positively employees will react to change initiatives and exhibit OCBs.

A Dissenting View of OCB

As popular as the concept of OCB implications are on employee engagement of change, it has had some degree of criticism. Because OCB is voluntary behavior, not mandated by formal directives or expectations, theorists have concluded that the informal organization is most influential in promoting workplace OCB (Levine, 2010). Although OCB is generally conceptualized as a positive aspect of organizational culture, studies suggest that under certain circumstances OCB may not be advantageous in achieving organizational goals (Kanihan et al., 2013; Pearce, 2010). This is especially so when stated organizational goals are undermined by individuals in the informal structure who have competing goals, such as dominant coalitions.

Dominant coalitions are the elite in the organization's social networks that wield extensive influence on organizational decision-making (Kanihan et al., 2013; Mulnix, Cojanu, & Pettine, 2011). When these coalitions are driven by positive motives, the coalitions enhance change. When they are driven by negative motives and leaders, change will be hindered. Dominant coalitions derive their power from the synergistic influence of its composite membership, which is generally inclusive of both formal and informal members. However, some surmise that coalitions tend to have a greater composite of members from the informal organizational structure.

The coalition power base is secured by their capacity to use their power and authority to drive the direction of decision related to goals and change initiatives (Kanihan et al., 2013; Mulnix et al., 2011; Pearce, 2010). Although primarily composed of informal leadership structures, dominant coalitions also include some top-level formal leaders. As a result, the decision-making influence of coalitions is often solidified by some level of formal support, which strengthens the coalition's authority. Because dominant coalitions often quietly drive many of the operational decisions within organizations, if the coalition is governed by negative informal leadership, this can be a detriment to the organization, resulting in the pursuit of self-interest and counter-productive behaviors.

Because OCB has become such a major focus of organizational study, research on counter-productive workplace behavior (CWB) research has also become a focus of research interest (Ahmad & Omar, 2013; Levine, 2010; Nair & Bhatnagar, 2011). Deviant behavior in the workplace has a number of labels to include counter-productive behavior, anti-social workplace behavior, workplace dysfunctionality, and maladaptive behavior. Whatever terminology is applied to the concept, the impact of workplace deviance has enormous impact on organizational risk and loss.

Workplace deviance is defined as any intentional actions that violate or undermine organizational norms or effectiveness (Ahmad & Omar, 2013). These behaviors, when allowed to continue unrestrained in the workplace, threaten the well-being of the organization and its stakeholder and detrimentally impact the bottom line. Studies have estimated that deviant workplace behavior causes organizational loss in the USA that range from $6 billion to $200 billion annually (Nair & Bhatnagar, 2011, p. 289).

The impact of the negative informal leader on the team is clearly evident in the study. Although the term *dominant coalition* was never discussed, what participants described in several instances was foundationally dominant coalitions. There were several instances when participants described groups within departments under the influence of a negative informal leader who had and used their connections with high-level formal leaders across the organization had wielded a great deal of influence in organizational decisions. These instances described supported strong social networks in which the negative leader would verbally acknowledge who they knew and what they could do because of that social connection. It is such long-standing behaviors and outcomes that directly influence an organization's overall culture that, although not documented, has significant impact on employee workplace behaviors.

6   Understand Workplace Culture

Management theorists, Robert Peters and Thomas Waterman, conducted pivotal research and established that organizational culture is one of the most important aspects of organizational success (Klein, 2011). As global competition increases, organizations are continuously seeking to employ strategies to maximize productivity and efficiency in the marketplace (Javadi & Ahmadi, 2013; Sarangi & Srivastava, 2012). Studies related to strategies to make that happen have been deeply rooted in understanding how to increase employee motivation within the workplace dynamic. Companies that have consistently applied strategies to get the most from their employees have been most successful in outpacing the competition. Studies within the last ten years have strongly suggested that organizational culture is a key determinant in promoting employee engagement, commitment, and satisfaction.

Culture Defined

Professor and industrial psychologist, Edgar Schein, conducted the germinal research studies related to how leaders create an organizational culture in which employees wanted to help leaders achieve organizational goals (Dimitrov, 2013; Kim & Mondello, 2014). He posited that culture is comprised of shared assumptions within a group dynamic. The vast array of empirical research conducted since that time has supported a strong correlation between organizational culture, performance, and effectiveness.

At the operational level, governing research described organizational culture as a composite of the informal rules that define and drive the general conduct of members of an organization (Mihaela & Bratianu, 2012;). This definition suggests that culture is rooted in the informal structure of an organization. Research also supports that culture represents the values that help members within an organization understand which of their actions are deemed acceptable or not acceptable within organizational norms. Values

DOI: 10.4324/9780429319969-7

are considered to be the intrinsic rational processes that prompt individuals to select, categorize, and apply meaning to environmental stimuli. It is through value perceptions that individuals make sense of their environment and the world around them, to include their workplace.

Organizational culture comprises the behavioral expectations of employees in the workplace and the expected way of getting things done (Kim & Mondello, 2014; Mihaela & Bratianu, 2012; Sarangi & Srivastava, 2012). At the work level, the concept encompasses the norms that define how work is done and what is expected during the work process. Creation of culture is a multifaceted paradigm which begins with perceptions of senior leadership behaviors and actions. The additional influencing factors include employee perceptions of workplace interactions, how challenges are dealt with, how stakeholders are treated, and other interpersonal activities. In strategizing to achieve maximum organizational success, the most successful leaders capitalize on the power that exists in a strong, positive corporate culture.

A strong, positive culture reduces collective uncertainties for team members, produces social order that clearly expresses member expectations, establishes continuity that promotes critical values and norms, creates a collective identity that members can relate to and embrace, and clarifies a corporate vision that energizes forward movement (Javadi & Ahmadi, 2013; Mihaela & Bratianu, 2012; Sarangi & Srivastava, 2012; Stebbins & Dent, 2011). In essence, the concept of culture defines how things are done in a work environment as well as drive the foundation of how employees' behaviors, actions, and attitudes create organizational norms (Klein, 2011).

Schein's Model Examined

With all the dialogue and research concerning organizational culture, it is still a rather abstract concept and difficult for many in leadership positions to understand. Edgar Schein's Organizational Culture model is accepted as the accepted business model for understanding how cultures develop (Dimitrov, 2013; Javadi & Ahmadi, 2013; Schein, 2010). In his research, he endeavored to help leaders understand how the concept culture can influence the actions, behaviors, and performance of employees, and the result of culture on behavior and performance outcomes.

Schein defines culture as the outcome of what group members learn over an extended period as members interact to solve its external problems of survival and its internal dilemmas of integration (Dimitrov, 2013; Schein, 2010). He maintained that as group members spend time together, they will engage in shared experiences that will result in a unique culture through cognitive behavioral and emotional processing (Javadi & Ahmadi, 2013; Kim & Mondello, 2014; Schein, 2010). As group members interact and process through various issues, concerns, or activities, cognitive processes will begin to connect aspects of the group dynamic that forge a bond in how group members interact. These cognitive processes determine how the group perceives who they are, their reality; how they embrace and advocate for certain values; and how they will address problems, both internal and external.

Schein further assessed that in the workplace, organizational culture is the shared value and belief systems that group members adopt as they process through the learning process that drive how group members behave in the workplace (Dimitrov, 2013; Gijselaers et al., 2011; Javadi & Ahmadi, 2013; Kim & Mondello, 2014; Schein, 2010). He assessed that organizational culture is not a short-term development process. The paradigm occurs as changes occur in the group, as group members adapt to the external environment, and as they resolve problems and issues that arise. Once organization culture develops, it will drive the way individuals interact with one another, how they respond to conflict, and how they see and engage with the organization (Mouton, Just, & Gabrielsen, 2012).

Schein's model of organizational culture outlines three elements that align to create the foundation in which cultures manifest (Dimitrov, 2013; Schein, 2010). The levels include artifacts, values, and assumptions. *Artifacts* are best defined as the tangible, observable, and identifiable attributes of the organization that provides the initial impression of what the organization is all about to internal and external constituents. Examples include objects within the organization and what those objects inspire in terms of behavior, such as physical architecture, workplace design, floor layout and spacing, furniture, ambience, and dress code. These are the first thing individual see, feel, sense, touch, or hear when they come in contact with the organization. The most difficult task related to artifacts is assuring that external observer interprets the artifacts the way the organization intends.

The second level of cultural model development is *values*, which are the organization's declared rules governing behavior (Dimitrov, 2013; Schein, 2010). These are the fundamental beliefs that influence or motivate attitudes, actions, and behaviors of employees. Values may be expressed in the organization's mission, vision, and core values. Schein points out that when individual values are consistent with the underlying beliefs and assumptions, employees will begin to embrace a philosophy of thinking and behaving in a manner that becomes integrated in group member norms. Through this process, the organization's identity will begin to emerge, which will begin to drive how the organization operates and how stakeholders interact. Senior leaders must not only ensure desired values are clearly stated but also that values are emulated consistently from the top–down.

The third level of the organizational culture model is *assumptions*. Assumptions are unexamined convictions or deep-seeded beliefs that are conceived within the organization without critical assessment (Dimitrov, 2013; Schein, 2010). In essence, they are unspoken rules of engagement and shared beliefs of the collective whole. Assumptions are the principal source of dominant values that employees embrace that drive integrated behavior that is the foundation of corporate culture. These drivers are silently understood actions that can make or break organizational success. Examples of assumptions that drive positive employee behavior include employees feeling they are valued and appreciated, or believing that the organization values honesty and open communication. Examples of assumptions that promote negative employee behaviors include employees believing they are not valued by leaders, or that they have to look out for themselves.

These three levels define how culture develops. Each level is often referred to as subcultures. Schein believes that the aligning these three subcultures is critical for organizational growth and to solidify how employees connect to the organization (Dimitrov, 2013; Schein, 2010). He assesses that many problems and issues that exist in organizations are the result of the disconnects among these levels. His model reveals that systemic and consistent work is critical to creating a culture that is advantageous to organizational growth. The outer layer, level one, artifacts, is easy to see and is thus easy to facilitate change. The deeper the layer, the more work is involved in accessing, understanding, and changing the paradigm. The deepest level, assumptions, is the most difficult to define and the most difficult to change.

Culture and Change Strategy

In the process of assessing the current culture and potentially facilitating change, several factors must be considered to impact the subcultures that define cultural development (Mouton et al., 2012; Shim, 2010). The greatest influencers in the process are organizational leadership and the mindset they bring to the leadership role. Leaders are positioned to influence all three levels of development: artifacts, values, and assumptions. Leadership character, style, and approach lay the foundation that determines whether the culture is positive, toxic, or indifferent, and whether the foundation is focused on growth or is stagnant. Research supports that leaders in organizations influence five target areas that impact cultural development, including vision and mission clarity, collaboration, staff development, resource allocation, and professional development.

Leaders are critical in assuring that stakeholders know and have clarity concerning the *vision and mission* of the organization on a consistent basis (Mouton et al., 2012; Shim, 2010). Employees must understand and embrace corporate vision and mission. These key elements serve as the focal point for laying the foundation for the organization and a road-map for stakeholders to follow. The vision statement describes the organization's ultimate goals, providing a mental image of the long-term desired future of where the organization is going. The mission statement is focused on the organization's current goals and objectives, outlining what the organization does and how it operates in the present. The vision is focused on the organization's future state; the mission is on the current state. If these concepts are not clearly codified and understood, employees will not be able to align with the leadership to help the organization achieve long-term goals.

Leaders must embody *collaboration* by encouraging and emulating working together towards goal achievement (Mouton et al., 2012; Shim, 2010). In laying the foundation for a strong positive culture, they must ensure employees do not feel that the leader alone is credited with all that goes well with the organization and getting things done. He or she must ensure that team members are not treated at any level as though they are dispensable. When employees feel that if they are easily replaceable, prosocial behaviors are minimized or eliminated in staff interactions. Collaboration in the organization does not just happen by accident. Leaders must purposely seek to establish a culture of collaboration. That is the foundation upon which organizational citizenship behaviors (OCBs) are enhanced, especially related to altruism and courtesy.

Leaders must provide avenues for *staff training and development* to encourage personal and professional growth (Mouton et al., 2012; Shim, 2010). Leaders have the overall responsibility of defining the strategic directions of the organization and determining how to monitor progress to assure goals are achieved in accordance with set timelines. Thus, it is essential that leaders define what organizational success will look like in order to assure a foundation of clarity in establishing a staff development strategy. In the process, must perceive there is employ equity in how the staff development strategy is planned and executed. When employees perceive that leaders care about them and their future as well as the organization, they will more willingly engage in pro-social behaviors, enhancing OCBs. Additionally, employees will have a stronger perception of distributive and procedural organization justice, which will lead to a more trusting leader-member exchange (LMX) relationship.

Employees expect leaders to assure they have *adequate resources* needed to do their job in a safe and productive work environment (Mouton et al., 2012; Shim, 2010). They have an unspoken confidence that they will bring the knowledge and skill needed to perform given tasks, and the organization will provide the resources for them to get the job done. Resources in an organizational context include any asset that can be used by an individual to perform or function effectively and complete tasks or projects. If resource shortages occur on a regular basis, employees will perceive negatively on the currencies of the LMX as well as a high sense of organizational injustice, lower pro-social behaviors, and low exhibition of OCBs. Leaders must effectively manage resource allocations to assure capacity to achieve organizational goals.

Finally, employees expect leader to provide *professional development* opportunities not only to help them improve the quality of their job performance on the job but also to aid in expanding their skills for the overall professional growth (Mouton et al., 2012; Shim, 2010). Research supports that if employees perceive their organization is not willing to invest in their future, they will seek other career opportunities. A vast majority of employees state that the lack of career development in the organizational paradigm would be sufficient to seek new employment. When employees feel their goals matter to the organization, they exhibit higher quality LMX relationships, positive perceptions of organizational justice, and more pro-social behaviors and OCBs.

Leaders must strive to create a positive foundation for cultural development that maximizes stakeholder success and minimizes stress in the workplace (Mouton et al., 2012; Shim, 2010). As the foundation is established, the stability and consistency of workplace interactions influence the strength of cultural development. Over time, the shared experiences based on leader-follower interactions, verbal and non-verbal messaging, and the strength and consistency of messages will become the organizational culture. In order to incept change in any deep-seeded cultural paradigm, Schein suggests an in-depth assessment must be conducted to determine the underlying causes of the dysfunction that led to the current cultural state. Stakeholders should be clearly informed of the need for change with clear goals and tactical steps related to what the transformation process will entail. Leaders must have a clear understanding that before a desired change can be expected, old patterns of behavior must be unlearned.

Classification of Organizational Cultures

Individuals from diverse backgrounds and various interests converge to form a work unit to achieve targeted goals in a platform called "the organization". How staff engage with each other, perform tasks, and embrace organizational norms depends upon the organizational culture. Several theorists have endeavored to explain the kinds of cultures in today's workplace (Mihaela & Bratianu, 2012; Stebbins & Dent, 2011). However, two models have gained more popularity in organizational research and deemed valid and reliable concepts. Cooke's Model of Organizational Culture identifies three distinct paradigms that impact the overall employee engagement. Quinn and Cameron's Organizational Culture Assessment identifies four possible cultural mixes in organizational operations. Each of these models provides a strong foundation of information for leadership consideration.

Cooke's Model of Organizational Culture

Organizational development guru and scholar, Dr. Robert Cooke, proposed that when employees come into a work environment, they conform to a pattern of behavior that they feel is the best posture to help them survive for the long term (Kim & Mondello, 2014; Klein, 2011; Javadi & Ahmadi, 2013; Stebbins & Dent, 2011). Employees get those queues from the existing culture. Cooke's Model of Organizational Culture classifies three distinct cultures as constructive, aggressive-defensive, or passive-defensive.

Creating a *constructive organizational culture* (COC) is a culture of positive norms and work values (Kim & Mondello, 2014; Mihaela & Bratianu, 2012). This culture, also known as affiliative, positively influences organizational growth, strategic direction, quality product or service delivery, employee engagement, and ultimate market success. It encourages members to interact with each other in a collaborative manner, fostering constructive interpersonal relationships. Tasks within this paradigm are characterized by achievement, a focus on self-actualization; humanistic encouragement; and affiliative engagement. Achievement encompasses members setting challenging but realistic goals. Self-actualizing in work comprises how members enjoy their work, take initiative, and engage in tasks. Humanistic-encouraging denotes supportive and helpful interactions. Finally, affiliative engagement signifies cooperative and collaborative teamwork.

In the *aggressive-defensive organizational culture* (ADOC), members are compelled to approach work expectations in a forceful manner, focused on protecting their status and security (Kim & Mondello, 2014; Mihaela & Bratianu, 2012). The culture is characterized by power, competitive, and perfectionist norms. This culture is based on positional power, conflict promotion, and rewarding negativity among the ranks. Senior members receive accolades for controlling behaviors that keep subordinates in compliant positions. This organizational paradigm values perfectionism and hard work but tends to undermine attempts at team collaboration in deference to individual achievement. Members within the organization are expected to work long hours to achieve assigned tasks with little encouragement to employ initiative or innovation. Ultimately, the goal tends to be maintaining the status quo with those in power positions to ensure that they remain in those positions.

The *passive-defensive organizational culture* (PDOC) is characterized by members' beliefs that work interactions must be non-threatening so as not to compromise job security (Kim & Mondello, 2014; Mihaela & Bratianu, 2012). Members tend to avoid conflict situations and seek approval of those in more authoritative positions. In this culture, members rarely employ creativity or introduce innovative ideas for fear of provoking supervisory disapproval or disagreement. Employees in the PDOC are careful to adhere to rules and policies, focusing primarily on task accomplishments, often at the expense of promoting customer service and client satisfaction. The environment tends to be traditional and bureaucratic with centralized decision-making. The cultural paradigm does not encourage participation, engagement, or team collaboration, and readily punishes mistakes and failures.

Quinn and Cameron's Organizational Culture Assessment

Business professors Robert Quinn and Kim Cameron proposed that although every organization has a unique dominant culture, every organization has the potential to have some mix of the four identified cultures as defined by their Organizational Culture Assessment Instrument (OCAI) (Barth, 2002; Kim, 2014; Mouton et al., 2012). The OCAI framework classifies organizational cultures into four distinct cultural types: the Clan, the Adhocracy, the Market, and the Hierarchy. The identified cultures are summarized as follows.

In the *Clan culture*, members have shared values and see themselves as part of a big family (Kim, 2014; Mouton et al., 2012). The values that are most honored and active are teamwork, communication, consensus, and compromise. Leaders focus on mentoring staff through interpersonal connections to build a stronger foundation of devotion and dedication to the "family". They seek to create and maintain a nurturing environment in which all members are active, involved, and do things together in an effort to encourage employee loyalty and high engagement. The Clan culture is rooted in collaboration and relationships. A major advantage of this culture is with a well-planned strategy, change can be more easily embraced because employees have a strong foundation of trust in leadership decision-making.

In the *Hierarchy culture*, the environment is formal, governed by strict procedural guidelines to direct employee work processes (Kim, 2014; Mouton et al., 2012). The values that are important are bureaucracy, stability, timeliness, and uniformity with an emphasis on control and structure. Operations are highly structured, procedures are well defined, and employees are mandated to stay in compliance. Leadership strategy involves strict monitoring of processes and work activities and ensuring efficiency, consistency, and predictability. In this culture, decision-making resides at the top with C-suite leaders. As a result, employees at lower levels often feel undervalued and powerless. So, although this structure often leads to more efficiencies, it does not lend itself to employee engagement, creativity, or innovative change.

In the *Market culture*, results are the main focus (Kim, 2014; Mouton et al., 2012). The work environment is united by a common goal to succeed and beat the competition. Competition is strongly encouraged with a focus on achieving results and getting things done. Leaders are tough, demanding, and highly goal driven with high expectations of the employees. Employees are expected to continually bring their A-game, competition is emphasized, and winners are rewarded. Goals are generally related to sales, profits, market position, stock value, and bottom-line corporate performance. The main values include market share and profitability. This paradigm will generally make it difficult to work together collaboratively on important projects. Change in this culture will not be impossible, but there will be difficulties because of the potential lack of workplace collaboration.

In the *Adhocracy culture*, employees are hired and encouraged to be dynamic, energetic, and creative (Kim, 2014; Mouton et al., 2012). This is the environment that accepts risk taking and encourages innovation. The values most honored are change, agility, and innovation. Leaders are seen as innovators who create an entrepreneurial atmosphere for staff because their goal is to be the first to market with whatever is being developed. Being first to market with new products or services defines organizational success. In this less structured culture, brainstorming sessions are promoted, and all employees are encouraged to participate regardless of position to promote the free flow of ideas. The environment is well suited to individuals who think outside the box and are comfortable making things happen. This environment is in a constant state of change due to the risk taking and encouraged creative posture of the organization. Change is generally eagerly embraced.

During their research, Quinn and Cameron assessed that organizations generally have a dominant culture and very rarely will have equal traits of all four cultural types (Kim, 2014; Mouton et al., 2012). However, it is possible that departmental units within an organization will have a culture that is counter to the primary organizational culture. For instance, an organization that has an adhocracy organizational culture might have an accounting department that is a hierarchy due to the need for tight financial controls. If change is desired in the organization, although defining the driving culture is difficult, leaders must take time to analyze why the company is where it is. Assessing the cultural position helps determine gaps between the current culture and the desired culture to determine the strategies for effective change.

In this study, the negativity of the culture was considered a primary reason for a negative informal leader's ability to continue to disrupt the team. Such a culture was not deemed conducive to promoting interpersonal relationships or information sharing among team members. Effectiveness in team operations mandates that team members be able to maximize knowledge sharing and team interactions, both of which were hindered according to participants.

7 Effective Change Management

It is often said that the only constant in the universe is change. Failed change initiatives and projects mean huge organizational losses for executives, leadership shortcomings for managers, and demotivation for employees (Hashim, 2013; Stoltzfus et al., 2011). Change is the cornerstone of organizational growth. However, it is also one of the most difficult tasks for leaders to achieve. In this age of global competition and advancing technologies, no organization can afford to remain stagnant. Organizations must employ strategies to address the hindrances and lay a foundation to make change happen smoothly and effectively. This is one area in which an informal leader can be the key to unlock the door to success or the roadblock to forward movement.

If a strong informal leader with referent power expresses serious concerns about how a proposed change might disrupt the team or negatively impact the work, team member engagement can be immediately undermined. Leaders who acknowledge how such influence can hinder change plans are cognizant of how these individuals can make or break a change objective. With change being a challenge in the best of circumstances, empowered leaders must be mindful of any element that might further challenge making change happen.

The Pace of Change Challenge

Change management is a systematic process of applying knowledge, tools, and resources to strategically initiate and usher a cultural shift in attitudes, expectations, productivity, and opportunities to meet strategic goals and objectives. The pace of change in the work environment is more rapid today than ever before (van der Voet, 2014; Vakola, 2013). The statistics for failure of change initiatives in public and private entities range between 65% and 75% (Jacobs, Rouse, & Parsons, 2014). With such high failure rates, leaders must position themselves to be more adaptable in the way they conduct business and facilitate change strategies.

DOI: 10.4324/9780429319969-8

Although disruptions are a norm when changes occur, it is important that leadership minimize disruptions during times of transition. In today's economic environment where resources are limited and cash flows are not always sufficient, the goal must be to gain buy-in and acceptance of change as quickly as possible with minimal disruption to operations (Hashim, 2013; Stoltzfus et al., 2011; Vakola, 2013; van der Voet, 2014). Employees are beset with overwhelming and often disruptive transformative mandates that must be implemented with efficiently within specified timeframes. How to obtain that level of engagement continues to be of major concern to leaders as well as the subject of numerous research studies (Hansen et al., 2014).

Failure of any organizational change initiative that negatively influences strategy for organizational success is cause for leadership concern (Battilana, Gilmartin, Sengul, Pache, & Alexander, 2010; Hashim, 2013). It is, therefore, important that leaders position themselves to be more adaptable in the way they conduct business and facilitate change strategies. As change incites negative responses that impact operations, gaining employee buy-in and acceptance of change are areas in which leaders continue to struggle, especially as it relates to changes in the leadership structure.

Effective Change Strategy

One of the most common questions that senior leaders ask is how long will it take for a change initiative to manifest (Jick, 1995)? Implementing change successfully mandates that leaders have a sound knowledge of what is desired (strategy), apt capabilities to facilitate and continually manage the new change state (competencies), and the short- and long-term tools to support the changed state (structure) (Battilana et al., 2010; van Knippenberg, 2011). If strategy, competencies, and structure are not properly aligned, the desired outcomes will not be achieved.

When these initiatives result in only short-term gains or consistent setbacks, the organization will revert to original behaviors (Battilana et al., 2010; Hashim, 2013; Hechanova & Cementina-Olpoc, 2013). Such fluctuations will eventually lead to employees discounting change announcements as frivolous and of no value. Thus, the empowered leader must not only determine what change is needed for the organization but also determine the most effective strategy for implementation of change processes.

Effectuating an effective change strategy takes time and a strategic focus on helping employees relinquish and unlearn old habits and adopt and engage new habits (Brisson-Banks, 2010; Jick, 1995; Kanihan, Hansen, Blair, Shore, & Myers, 2013; Pardo-del-Val, Martínez-Fuentes, & Roig-Dobón, 2012). Although communication is crucial to any successful change initiative, the difficult decisions related to positioning the organization for change success must be made prior to rolling out an organizational communication. In crafting an effective communication strategy, leaders must be cognizant of assuring the appropriate resource availabilities at the time of the change announcement.

How leaders introduced and communicated a planned change initiative is deemed a critical component of setting the right tone for employee engagement or rejection of the change effort (Hechanova & Cementina-Olpoc, 2013; Pardo-del-Val et al., 2012; Simoes & Esposito, 2014). An effective communication strategy is purposed to increase organizational awareness, reduce resistance, and prepare employees for how change affects organizational operations. A clear, honest communication of change strategy not only encompasses what is said or written but also includes the actions leaders take during the change process. Followers must see progressive actions that promote engagement and exhibit consideration for what followers endure during the change initiative.

Although some change initiatives can be facilitated quickly, adjusting to most change takes time (Hashim, 2013; Pardo-del-Val et al., 2012; Shirey, 2013). To maximize success, the prudent leader should employ a participative management style to engage followers to embrace the initiative and pursue change as a series of strategic steps to help followers adjust to the change effort slowly for greater support. Seeking to facilitate change too quickly or through ineffective implementation can result in lower productivity, poor customer service, and low morale. Ultimately, ineffective implementation and communication strategy will result in failed change directives. Jick (1995) asserted that the three areas that present the greatest opportunities to accelerate change successfully include assuring a clear understanding of change goals, taking actions consistent with desired outcomes, and maintaining momentum. These actions aid in employees making the psychological transition to the new change paradigm (Brisson-Banks, 2010).

The Psychology of Change

Change management research supports that making the psychological transition to the new paradigm is the component of change that causes most issues with change initiatives (Bouckenooghe, 2010; Brisson-Banks, 2010). Two of the biggest mistakes leaders make during a change paradigm that undermine change success are failure to clearly communicated what the change entails and expecting individuals to adjust to changes too quickly. Once the change initiative has been aptly communicated, individuals affected by change must be afforded time to make the psychological transition associated with each step in the change process.

The psychological transition process involves employees aligning the desired organizational action with employee's individual perceptions of what the change means to him or her and trusting that the desired change is not intended for the employee's detriment (Brisson-Banks, 2010; Stoltzfus et al., 2011). Transitioning to the desired state of change successfully requires employees to release old expectations (disorientation) and embrace new paradigms for growth (reorientation). When employees perceive that organizational leaders are psychologically committed to them as stakeholders, the transitioning process is more easily embraced, and employees will be more committed to the change goal.

Change management research supports that a significant change initiative may be hindered if the change climate is low (Du & Choi, 2013; Hashim, 2013; Hechanova & Cementina-Olpoc, 2013; Stoltzfus et al., 2011). An organization's change climate signifies the perception employees have of how diligently organizational leaders encourage and support innovation and change in the culture as evidenced by the policies, practices, and procedures. The perception is generally based on the social interactions within work groups and how messages of change are communicated throughout the organization. Thus, it is important for leaders to prepare organizations for change before change is introduced. Exactly how organizational readiness is to be achieved and to what extent organizations facilitate this directive successfully is another arena of change for which little empirical evidence exist (Du & Choi, 2013; Vakola, 2013).

Organizational readiness is a complex paradigm whereby leaders seek to assess if stakeholders have a desire to see change manifested (change commitment) and if employees perceive they have the capacity and competence to implement the desired change directive (collective efficacy) (Lin & Peng, 2010; Vakola, 2013). When change commitment and collective efficacy are high, stakeholders are positioned to initiate action, exert needed effort to achieve success, persevere through setbacks, and exhibit greater collaboration and cooperation. When commitment and efficacy are low, organizations are not well positioned for change, which increases the potential for failure. Organizational readiness represents stakeholder psychological agreement to embrace change and put forth the effort to help the organization succeed (Vakola, 2013). Readiness is hindered when leaders are ineffective in implementing strategic change processes before attempting to introduce a major change initiative.

Change Management Theory

There are a number of change management models that have garnered note as creditable by leading change management theorist. However, two of the most impacting theories related to effective change in the organizational paradigm include Lewin's three-stage model and Kotter's eight-step model of change.

Lewin's Three-Stage Model

To fully understand the concept of change as it relates to workplace interactions, theoretical models must be discussed. One of the most fundamental change management theories is Lewin's three-stage model (Lewin, 1951; Shirey, 2013; Worley & Mohrman, 2014). Kurt Lewin is a social psychologist known as one of the leading pioneers of social, organizational, and applied psychology in the workplace. His change management model has been deemed one of the best methodologies to usher a platform of organizational readiness with an emphasis on unfreezing existing behaviors to eliminate old habits to lay a foundation for desired change.

Lewin proposed that change strategy requires three stages to effectuate long-term, lasting change: unfreeze, mobilize, and refreeze (Lewin, 1951; Shirey, 2013; Worley & Mohrman, 2014). In essence, Lewin proposed that the process of effective change requires a strategy to communicate the critical need for a change initiative, then usher followers towards the desired (new) behaviors, and, finally, solidify the new behaviors and activities as the new organizational norm. The three-stage model posited that change is a linear, straightforward process that is driven from the senior levels of management and requires consistency in leadership actions. The model focuses on a leader's role and responsibility in creating a foundation of urgency for a pending change initiative to move change forward.

During stage 1, the unfreeze stage, leaders must create a business case that is clearly communicated to followers and that highlights why current circumstances are a source of dissatisfaction and needs to change (Lewin, 1951; Shirey, 2013; van der Voet, 2014; Worley & Mohrman, 2014). The unfreeze process challenges existing organizational beliefs, clarifies the change vision, and creates a core excitement for the change initiative. Stage 2, mobilization, involves identifying and mobilizing needed resources to manifest the desired change. It is also critical that followers perceive they have what they need to ensure the success of the change initiative. Resource availabilities include manpower, knowledge, competencies, machinery, technology, and finances needed to produce desired outcomes. If followers feel that they do not have critically needed resources to do what is needed, their commitment to the change will be lessened.

Refreezing, stage 3, involves implementing new tactics, methodologies, and strategies to create new norms for organizational operations (Lewin, 1951; Shirey, 2013; van der Voet, 2014; Worley & Mohrman, 2014). It is the process of fortifying, stabilizing, and solidifying the change as the new organizational norm. Throughout the linear process of change implementation, Lewin emphasizes the critical role of leadership in engaging followers to maximize success. This model has been criticized as being too simplistic for real-world applications; however, the theory is still one of the most prevalent in change management practice.

Kotter's Eight-Step Model

Kotter's model for transforming organizations is a second widely incepted platform for organizational change (Lawler & Sillitoe, 2010). Dr. John Kotter is a professor of leadership at the Harvard Business School and considered one of the foremost authorities (a thought leader) in business, leadership, and change. His model suggests that leaders must first lay a strong foundation to convince followers of an urgent need for change action to get buy-in (Battilana et al., 2010; Kotter, 1995; Lawler & Sillitoe, 2010). The eight-step model is premised upon the concept that change is manifested through a series of phases that require an investment of time and that critical errors in any particular phase can be detrimental to change momentum or success.

Step 1 in the Kotter model is aligned with the core strategy of Lewin's model, which is to *create a sense of urgency* for desired change (Kotter, 1995; Lawler & Sillitoe, 2010). This step requires leaders to connect to followers by communicating with definitive, bold, honest statements that emphasize that the change need is urgent. Creating a sense of urgency helps inspire employees to willingly embrace the change goals and encourage continued engagement for progressive action. A major reason change initiatives fail is due to organizational leader's underestimation of individuals' reactions, responses, and interactions. To minimize this potential, step 2 of the model, Kotter proposed the need to *form strong coalitions* that will continually advocate for the change (Kotter, 1995; Lawler & Sillitoe, 2010). The process involves identifying key stakeholders who can serve as coalition leads to promote follower commitment to the needed change. These coalitions should be composed of as many influential individuals from across the organization to work as teams on specific areas of focus in the change process.

In step 3, organizations must *create a clear vision* of what is desired, framed so that everyone at every level can easily understand what is being asked of them (Kotter, 1995; Lawler & Sillitoe, 2010). In this process, emphasis should be given to defining core values and ensuring clarity in helping employees see the vision of what the change will do for the organization as well as for employees. Leaders must make it easy for employees to see and follow. In an effort to ensure this happens, step 4 is critical. Leaders must *communicate the vision*, which is focused on ensuring the vision is clearly and consistently communicated so that employees understand how critical the change is to organizational operations (Kotter, 1995; Lawler & Sillitoe, 2010). This involved communicating to employees in different ways with a powerful, honest, and convincing message that connects the vision to performance, training, organizational and employee interest, etc.

If an organization successfully reaches step 5, Kotter suggested that the organization must focus on *removing obstacles* (Kotter, 1995; Lawler & Sillitoe, 2010). By this time in the change plans, leader should have successfully conceptualized all potential contingencies. If in the communication process, there were hints or warning signs of dissension or divisiveness, leader must take quick action to decisively remove obstacles to ensure change momentum is not impeded. The organization must implement ways to monitor for barriers or signs of resistance and implement proactive measures to address the obstacle. In step 6, leaders will want to *create short-term wins* (Kotter, 1995; Lawler & Sillitoe, 2010). Creating and acknowledging short-term wins will provide spurts of inspiration to keep the momentum moving and help promote a sense of success in the momentum. Celebrating the short-term success and those who were important in achieving each short-term accomplishment is an excellent way to minimize negativity while maintaining motivation for change outcomes.

While it is important to promote short-term wins, Kotter supports that leaders must also *consolidate gains*, step 7 (Kotter, 1995; Lawler & Sillitoe, 2010). It is important to ensure that celebrating the short-term wins does not distract from the end goal of the change initiative. This requires building upon each win to identify what is going well, determine what needs to improve in order to maintain momentum, and ensure a continued focus on the goal. Finally, in step 8, leaders must *anchor the change in the corporate culture* (Kotter, 1995; Lawler & Sillitoe, 2010). Kotter maintained that change must become imbedded in the organizational culture for the change to be complete. In essence, the change must be exhibited and reinforced in every aspect of daily work and in leadership behaviors to deter resistance, infuse change in employee behavior, and assure employees do not revert to old patterns.

Kotter's model provides a clear path to implement change in a step-by-step approach (Lawler & Sillitoe, 2010). It has been deemed an easy process to implement which provides tactical strategies upon which organization can benchmark success. The model emphasizes the role of leadership in assuring employee engagement throughout the process. Kotter's approach clearly reveals how important informal leadership engagement might be in laying a foundation for change engagement or change resistance.

Change Management Execution

Change management (CM) is a term for the overall approach to formulate an organizational strategy to help incept a shift or transition on some or all levels of organizational operations. (Hashim, 2013; Vakola, 2013). Based on the prevalence of change in the workplace, an effective change management execution process requires a wholistic focus and strategic assessment of the internal and external environment, sufficiency of organizational resources, apt technology capacity, a detailed communication strategy, and strong stakeholder support. Leaders involved in executing the change strategy must tactically assess how employees will fit into change management planning. It is critical that the right individuals are in the right place with the right skills to make the change happen.

Change in any organizational paradigm is a challenging, intense, and frustrating process. It is critical that two elements, early communication and change-oriented education, are facilitated early to engage stakeholder support of the initiative (Vakola, 2013). Unfortunately, these two elements are often the last components to receive targeted attention during the change process. However, these components are imperative to laying the foundation for change support and to overcome early resistance to change initiatives.

Stakeholder Engagement

Stakeholder engagement is mandatory for change initiative success. When stakeholders, especially employees who are impacted by the change, are not engaged to make the change happen, there is increased propensity to reject change efforts (Bankar & Gankar, 2013; Bringselius, 2014). Disengaged employees who are essential to executing initiatives will be a major detriment to success. Effective execution of a change management initiative encompasses five important stages to lay the foundation for full engagement of stakeholder, including understanding, belief and acceptance, caring and concern, planning, and implementation. Each stage must be facilitated proficiently to assure the change efforts transfer to routine activities of employees.

In stage 1, leaders must ensure understanding of the change initiative (Bringselius, 2014). Understanding is defined as acquiring a foundation of knowledge and/or familiarity with a particular thing or acquiring a skill in dealing with or handling the context of something. This stage includes helping stakeholders understand why the change is necessary, what the change steps will look like, a projected timeline, and identified key players.

In stage 2, belief and acceptance, leaders must show that they believe in the potential of the initiative to improve some level of organizational operations and that the change has value to improving some deficiency (Bringselius, 2014). This stage mandates clearly communicating to all impacted stakeholders at all levels, with a compelling case on how the change will influence each stakeholder as well as the positive influence on organizational operations. Leaders must also ensure adequate resources and time allocation to assure success.

In the caring and concern stage, stage 3, leaders must show care and concern for what stakeholders will have to endure in the process of incepting the change into the organizational culture (Bringselius, 2014). They must be able to exhibit compassion related to how each employee will be impacted by the change. This also involves providing any special training or educational needs necessary to ensure the skillsets and competencies of staff to assure capacity to perform in the midst of the new change.

The planning stage, stage 4, is focused on implementing the tactical strategy required to do what is needed for the change execution (Bringselius, 2014). Each organizational unit or component involved in the change effort should be given tactical expectations of that unit's responsibilities. These tactical steps include determining activities required for implementation, estimating time and resource requirements, determining parallel and sequential timeline, identifying and assessing how to mitigate risk factors, and determining and managing budgets.

In stage 5, the implementation stage, leaders must assure the right balance of staff resources with the necessary competencies to implement the change strategy (Bringselius, 2014). This includes effective monitoring of progress, making changes when and where needed, continually assessing risk factors, and continually assessing the climate to assure stakeholders stay engaged. To assure this balance, there must be frequent interactions with staff to talk about the change initiative, have status checks, and celebrate milestones along the way.

Change Resistance

Researchers have suggested that to gain a better understanding of resistance to change, one might conceptualize it as loss of something that one considers important (Bringselius, 2014; Bouckenooghe, 2010; Hashim, 2013; Shirey, 2013). The perception of potential loss will promote a posture of resistance, which can manifest as anger, fear, distress, irritation, denial, or negative attitudes. Resistance occurs when employees are uncertain of proposed change outcomes and when employees perceive that change will have negative effects. Such perceptual dissociation has been reported to result in decreased productivity, massive turnover, decreased work quality, deterioration in work relations, change myopia, and increased potential of organizational sabotage. These concepts converge to increase the potential for change to fail substantially.

Change interrupts the normal patterns of organizational behaviors and operations as well as challenges the status quo (Battilana et al., 2010; Bouckenooghe, 2010; Bringselius, 2014; Hechanova & Cementina-Olpoc, 2013). As a result, human resistance to change initiatives is often a major obstacle to successful change initiatives. Leaders must be able to help followers understand that maintaining the status quo is not in their best interest. Leaders must continually monitor the environment for any potential sources of resistance that may hinder engagement or encourage complacency and be prepared to cope with the issue.

The critical component of coping with resistance is that leaders to understand the psychological needs of those affected by the initiative (Battilana et al., 2010; Bouckenooghe, 2010; Nolan, 2010). It is important that they do not position as *change agent-centric* leaders, which supports that leaders believe change is only needed at the staff level. Most of the leaders do not consider that they, as individuals, are organizational entities that need to change. Thus, these leaders rarely consider themselves a source of hindrance to change efforts. Empowered leaders must consider all entities in planning and executing a change strategy, including themselves. An effective approach to understanding resistance must incorporate all dimensions of resistance to identify why change success rates are so low as well as how to best achieve desired outcomes.

Reasons Behind Resistance

Most of the leaders during a change initiative fail to acknowledge how these reasons for resistance influence follower behavior in the face of change (Bringselius, 2014). In order to assure that employees embrace change, empowered leaders must consider the causes behind resistance and seek to help employees align their fears with the realities of the change that must take place.

The most common reasons for resistance to change are based on how employees perceive the impact of the initiative on their lives (Battilana et al., 2010; Han & Harms, 2010; Hashim, 2013). Some of the most prevalent causes that employees resist change include fear of the unknown, concern for how the change will benefit or undermine their position, concern that the change will devalue their role in the organization, differing perspectives and perceptions about the impact of the change, a desire to remain with what is comfortable due to long-standing habits, and the fear of feeling inadequate to master the change.

Leaders must ensure that major change initiatives are not only well planned but also be well communicated at every level of the organization to aptly address any potential foundation of resistance. When change is not communicated well, the potential for failure and resistance is magnified. How leaders handle change initiatives is the key to engaging employees to align to achieve organizational goals related to change in the workplace. It is imperative that every resource be employed to ensure success in the change initiative. Aligning the informal leader to support the initiative is an effective strategy to help engage team members to the change goals.

Team Composite and Change

The team composite must be considered as change strategy is contemplated, especially when seeking to minimize resistance and maximize success (Johnson et al., 2013; Morita & Burns, 2014; Resick et al., 2010; Stoltzfus et al., 2011). Team members unwilling to embrace change can drastically hinder progress or may actively sabotage initiatives. Therefore, it is important that leaders fully understand the nature of change and how individuals in the work dynamic will respond to the concept of change. How team members respond to change can have an infectious outcome. If team members are engaged, they can create synergy and inspire creativity in each other in manifesting the change. If team members are disengaged, they can promote rigidity and greater resistance.

Because leaders and followers' posture from different perspectives, if team members do not clearly understand the leader's perspective, team members may perceive that the change poses a threat (DeOrtentiis et al., 2013; Nasomboon, 2014; Stoltzfus et al., 2011; van der Voet, 2014). If such a threat is perceived, team member may form a united alliance of resistance that could be difficult to overcome. By fully understanding how to best address team member perceptions, leaders can begin to help individuals transition to accept and embrace change more readily and as a result, gain team engagement more quickly.

8 Informal Leadership Influence on Engagement

This informal leadership study examined the role of the informal leader in promoting or hindering team member engagement of change initiatives as directed by formal leadership. Special emphasis was given to actions of integrating a new formal leader to the team composite. The relationship between the formal leader and the informal leader was explored to assess the relational impact on a formal leader's authority to execute leadership decisions as well as the relational influence on team citizenship behaviors in the team dynamic, especially as related to new formal leadership. The analysis involved assessing team members' perceptions of the formal and informal leaders' relationship as well as informal leadership influence on individual performance and on team cohesion.

The current study outcomes not only supported the germinal research that exists concerning informal leadership influence but also fully substantiated that informal leaders directly influence several organizational and team concepts that promote or hinder employee engagement and the success of change initiatives. The insights are helpful for recommending steps organizational leaders might take to increase team member engagement of a formal leader's initiatives in a changing environment.

Leadership Style on Informal Leader Authority

Although the research on the informal leader's influence in organizations is just becoming a major area of organizational development study, the germinal research facilitated thus far clearly supports these non-titled leaders do have authority. This research study supported that these individuals can wield a great deal of influence based on their perceived social power base dependent upon their charismatic personality (referent power), specialized knowledge (expert power), or organizational knowledge (information power).

The study also supported that an informal leader can be positive and enhance team operations, or negative and undermine the team dynamic.

DOI: 10.4324/9780429319969-9

Formal leaders will want to seek to capitalize on the presence of the informal leader but also be conscientious of the kind of influence the informal leader has on the culture of the team. However, not all leaders will find the process of engaging the informal leader an easy task because not all leaders will have the personality or interest in acknowledging or using the influence of informal leaders.

Transactional Leader and Informal Leader

Transactional leaders are unlikely to acknowledge or entertain any input from an informal leader because their focus is more process oriented than people oriented. The autocratic or authoritative leader is driven by command and control. They do not see their employees as team members, generally minimize interactions with subordinates, and are in no way interested in sharing power or authority. As a result, if any subordinate voices any dissenting views, they will very likely have to deal with the autocratic leader's coercive power to dispense some level of disciplinary action. The bureaucratic leader is driven by rules, regulations, and structured protocols. Although they will have some level of interaction with staff, they do so to maintain order, not with a focus on staff engagement. As a result, under bureaucratic leadership, employees are not inspired to do anything other than "their jobs". A strong informal leader will not be embraced with any measure of authority under either of these leadership styles.

Transformational Leader and Informal Leader

Transformational leaders are much more likely to acknowledge employees who exhibit social power influences of an informal leader. The democratic or participative leader encourages their team member to speak, share their ideas, and join in decision-making. This leadership style embraces what others on the team have to say. However, they maintain the authority to make the final decision. So, although they will be open to engaging an informal leader, they will generally only entertain a strong, vocal informal leader for so long. However, the delegative or permissive leader will gladly entertain a strong informal leader. This leader will easily surrender their authority to any seemingly strong team member who is interested. As a result, it will be easy for a strong informal leader to assume a position of influence within the team. However, there may be issues related to who is deemed the real leader of the team.

The empowered leader is open, not only to sharing power and authority but also to actively seeking engagement of all team members to be a part of the decision-making process. They are open to new ideas as well as inviting to those who have dissenting ideas, as they see such interactions as growth opportunities for all. Like the situational leader, they want to see positive informal leaders rise up in the team. They make it easy for the informal leader to wield much influence in the team with confidence that the informal leader will have a formal leader supporting their positive interactions and contributions.

New Formal Leader Entry

Study participants suggested that the formal leader was the benchmark on how team members perceived their value to the organization which promoted team members to engage or disengage. Team members tended to react more positively to leaders who exhibited an authentic leadership posture, exhibiting a strong sense of self-confidence while simultaneously ensuring connection to each team member. Team members also seemed to positively engage with leaders when they exhibited transparency in communication and interacting with the team. Transparency and the self-regulating aspect of authentic leadership was deemed especially important when new leaders entered the team composite. New formal leaders should be continuously mindful of failing to engage team members as quickly as possible upon assuming a formal leadership position. Failure to do so will hinder team building and change strategies.

New Leader and Informal Leader Assessment

When a new formal leader joined the team, participants reported that team members tended to adopt the attitude of the informal leader related to engaging the new leader. This was especially true for the positive informal leader with a strong foundation of referent or expert social power base. When the positive informal leader was open to a new leader, team members were eager to see what the formal leader would do to make the organization better. The informal leader's responses made team members more receptive and willing to give the formal leader a chance. With the support of this informal leader, a new formal leader was positioned to build a strong foundation for unified team operations from the onsite of their leadership journey.

If the formal leader was initially perceived as dictatorial or authoritative, the positive informal leader was instrumental in helping the formal leader understand the critical need to be more engaging and less authoritative when the formal leader was willing to listen. New formal leaders would be well served to understand the basic tenants of team development when a new team member is introduced to an existing team dynamic. Although, according to Tuckman's team development model, an introduction of a new team member may not revert the team to a forming stage, but there will invariably be elements of storming.

During storming, team members will have feelings of anxiety and expected unease due to the new addition to the team. This is particularly applicable when a new formal leader comes into the team composite. Team members reportedly responded with caution as they endeavored to understand the expectations of the new leader. This stage will generally result in team tensions and potential disagreement among individuals. Such a potential is greatly enhanced if the new leader is authoritative.

When the informal leader's attitude was more fearful of the unknown and unexcited about a new leader's entry to the team, team members emulated the informal leader's attitude and were somewhat restrained in welcoming the new leader. They were prone to trust the informal leader's assessment of the new leader, even in the absence of any supportive information to support the foundation of distrust. Team members had full confidence in the informal leader's intentions and trusted that informal leader had no selfish motives for their responses to the new leader. These findings suggest that the new formal leader should assess the team, identify the informal leader, and seek to positively engage the informal leader as a point of entry to the team as the team lead.

Formal Leader Authority

Study participants revealed that in the absence of a strong informal leader, team members were prone to embrace the new formal leader's authority from the new leader's entry to the team. They seemed more open to giving the new leader the benefit of the doubt and giving them a level of trust to see what the leader brings to the table. New formal leaders who exhibited empowered leadership with authentic leader characteristics consistently obtained positive feedback and responses from team members. Some team members were supportive of the new leader out of respect, while others specifically want to build a foundation for collaborative team operations. Many team members perceived that embracing the new leader in an engaging way helped enhance the team's image to the new leader.

If the formal leader was perceived as negative and there was no influential informal leader, employees responded to formal leadership directives out of respect alone for the formal leader's role but did not do so out of a desire to achieve team success. This response resulted in employees doing the bare minimum to comply to leadership directives but not engage the leader for relationship building. Participants also suggested that in cases of a strong negative formal leader, employees responded to the formal leader because of the fear of reprisal or due to the coercive power of leadership. This is generally the automatic response in a culture in which the perception of organizational justice is deemed unfair or inequitable, especially as related to distributive and procedural justice. Participants supported that in such team cultures, no one would consider challenging the formal leader based on the fear factor.

Participants cited a negative formal leader's leadership posture, communication style, and task focus as hindrances to employees bonding as a team under the new leadership. These leaders minimized their interactions with team members and created a perception that team members were not very important. They were authoritative in their behaviors, failed to effectively communicate, and did not take time to get to know team members. As a result, employees felt psychologically disconnected from the leader. If the organization's culture was also negative (organizational identity), it made it easier for team members to disconnect, become self-protective, and disengage.

Informal Leader Identification

According to research findings, it is sometimes difficult to identify the informal leader because the determination is based on how followers feel, what they think, the strength of relationships, and workplace interactions. This study supported the assertion that the informal leader was not easily identifiable. Thirty percent of participants had to think critically to identify an informal leader in the work group. A primary reason seemed to be due to participant's having given little forethought about the concept of an informal leader or their influence on the team until participation in this study and they thought about the definition of informal leadership.

New formal leaders should be mindful of making quick judgments as to who might have influence in the team without taking time to assess what is going on in the team dynamic. Even if the individual does not recognize their role as an informal leader, most existing teams will have an informal leader by virtue of personality, expertise, or longevity. Many informal leaders who have great respect and admiration on teams do not always realize the great influence they wield. However, new formal leaders cannot afford to overlook this critical resource.

New formal leaders should refrain from wearing the new formal title with expectations of immediate compliance and immediately facilitating any change actions without first monitoring team interactions. Study participants consistently stated that they did not feel the formal leaders took take time to get to know the team before making extensive changes. Such actions caused team members to respond with frustration, anger, and obstinacy because the formal leader took no time to build a foundation of trust, respect, or loyalty. By taking time to get to know team members as well identifying and engaging informal leaders, a new formal leader will be better positioned to understand the psychological needs of team members and effectively engage staff on a cognitive, emotional, and physical level. This will make the formal leader's job as team lead an easier transition.

The Positive Informal Leader

Informal leaders with positive traits reportedly were perceived as consistent sources of inspiration to team unity and advocated for working diligently to get the job done despite other prevailing issue. When informal leaders are open, respected, and trusted, team members tended to mimic their actions. According to past research, when team members like and respect a leader, team members more readily follow the leader, support leadership actions, and are more motivated to give of themselves. This research study supported that team members responded to the positive informal leader with that level of engagement, even if they did not agree with the informal leader. This, in essence, positioned the informal leader with more authority with team members than the formal leader.

When the formal leader gave a task directive, the positive informal leader was often the first to support that the team must do what was needed to complete the task, encouraging productive action from team members. The resultant actions from team members supported that there is a direct link between the informal leader's influence and an employee's productivity. Because of a foundation of trust in the informal leader's authentic leadership posture, team members were prone to do as the informal leader requested without question or doubt.

When positive informal leaders had something to say, team members were willing to listen, share, and communicate more openly with each other. According to Wheelan's integrated model of group development, communication and sharing are among the first traits required to begin the process of effective team building. The findings in the current study supported that the positive informal leader promoted a strong foundation of communication, collaboration, and unity – the benchmark of team development.

The Negative Informal Leader

Negative informal leaders were deemed to be of major concern to team members. Participants associated the negative informal leader with destructive work behaviors, undesirable work outcomes, and demotivating team culture. They were deemed duplicitous in that they would present themselves one way in front of the formal leader and were the complete opposite with the team when the leader was not around. These individuals were labeled self-serving, a disruption to the team, fault finding, and not having the best interest of the organization at heart. They would talk negatively about the organization and the formal leader, seeking to talk against the formal leader's directives and instructions. They often seem to take an opposite viewpoint of a change initiative, not out of conviction but just to be difficult.

These individuals were identified as purposeful rule-breakers, seeking to get others to support their ideas, which may be contrary to organizational standards. Unfortunately, participants supported that as much as 60% of staff would follow the lead of the negative informal leader, which caused team division. This was especially so if they had a strong personality (referent power), or they had longevity and were perceived as experts. Negative informal leaders with a strong social power base reportedly had the capacity to cause team division and inspired team members to mistrust and mistreat each other. They were deemed to be skilled at pitting employees and leaders against each other to achieve their personal agendas.

This informal leader's posture, attitude, and actions led to negative impact to team cognition, which resulted in individuals not freely sharing information with their fellow team members and undermined efforts to assure achievement of team goals. They additionally detrimentally influenced team mental models which undermined the team's mental capacity to see themselves as a unified body, maximize team interactions, or feel valued as a collaborative unit. They were perceived to purposefully promote conflict, discord, and a non-sharing culture. In the process, they made simple tasks difficult.

One of the biggest complaints of study participants was that the negative informal leader was allowed to spread seeds of discord and demotivation unhindered. Team members did not understand how anyone in a formal leadership position could allow someone with such destructive influence on the team to continue to wreak havoc and seemingly not make the individual behave according to expectation. By allowing such behavior to go unchecked, team members stated that they lost respect and trust not only for the formal leader but also for the organization. It resulted in team members psychologically disconnecting from the organization (weak organizational identity) and being less vested in helping promote organizational goals.

Although this leader had significant influence on the overall team's interaction, collaboration, and cognition, a significant number of participants reported that the negative informal leader's behaviors did not directly influence their individual performance efforts. This informal leader only seems to have influence at the individual level on employees who already exhibited negative personality traits. For these leaders with strong social influence, employees perceived that they were allowed to get away with things that others would be penalized for and as a result were seen as untouchable.

My experience in human capital management supports that in a negative work environment, individuals tend to stay true to their own character and work ethic when it comes to job performance. However, teamwork is more interactive, dependent upon influences outside of the individual. Even though individual work output and productivity are not significantly influenced by negative informal leaders, formal leaders must still be proactive in dealing with this negative leader because of the considerable detrimental influence on the overall team engagement and cognition.

Informal Leader and New Team Member Integration

Participants supported that positive informal leader served as a proponent to engage new people, consistently reminding the team to be mindful of first impressions and to present themselves in a way to engage new team members. They further supported that they believed that a negative informal leader seemed to be influenced by positivity when positive new people joined the team who did not buy in to negative posturing. When new people came into the team who were engaging, optimistic, helpful, friendly, and open to sharing, the negative informal leader tempered the negativity in their attitude and behaviors. Sometimes the change in the negative informal leader's behavior was for a short period of time, sometimes for a longer tenure.

If the new person was someone of stronger personality, and seemingly stronger influence, participants stated they would witness a transformation in the negative informal leader. This would suggest that a formal leader should actively monitor the skillset of new people brought into the team as well as assess their character traits. Additionally, these findings support a negative posture can change. Thus, formal leaders who assess the team has a negative team culture should proactively and aggressively seek to change the culture by focusing on infusing positivity into team interactions and proactively addressing negative team members, especially negative informal leaders.

Formal–Informal Leader Interactions

According to the social workplace contract, employees expect leaders to ensure they have what they need to adequately perform their job responsibilities as well as ensure that work conditions are conducive to working effectively. To that end, leaders must seek to create and maintain a supportive climate of collaboration and professionalism in interactions among team members. Failure to do so will result in a foundation of broken trust of the social workplace contract. Once that transpires, employees will disconnect and disengage. The primary interactive relationship that study participants supported influenced how team members viewed leadership was the relationship between the formal and informal leaders.

Positive Formal–Informal Leader Interactions

The study supported that the interaction between the formal and positive informal leader directly impacted the overall team relationships for the good of individual team members as well as for the team overall. Relationships were strengthened when the two leaders were open to communicating with each other and when they exhibited mutual respect. Team members viewed the formal leader with higher levels of respect when the formal leader was open to listening to the informal leader and was responsive to the informal leader's requests and concerns. This level of engagement encouraged team members to be comfortable in the team dynamic and more comfortable asking challenging questions. Because the relationships were strengthened and engagement was higher, the team embodied a constructive culture, which promoted team members to want to succeed in directives to please the formal leader and ensure team successes.

In situations in which the informal leader was positive with a strong foundation of social power, the informal leader had a significant amount of influence on team interactions as well as on influencing the formal leader interactions with the team. When concerns had potential negative impact, the formal leader was confident in support of the informal leader to aid in helping team members understand the formal leader's position. Because the formal leader was receptive to listening to the informal leader, the informal leader held high levels of respect for the formal leader and the formal leader's decisions. Team members likewise more easily embraced the formal leader's directives and decisions.

According to the feedback from the formal leadership interviews, when the relationship was positive, formal leaders actively pursued the informal leader's ideas and suggestions. They additionally supported that they were open to hearing what informal leaders had to say about various situations, not only with the team but also with other decisions for which the formal leader might be involved. The informal leader sometimes became a sounding board for the formal leader because of the high trust factor between the two. According to study participants, when team members observed such a relationship, the trust in the formal leader was magnified, which reduced any potential resistance from team members with any requests from the formal leader, including change initiatives.

Negative Formal–Informal Leader Interactions

Participant feedback supported that negative interactions between the formal and informal leaders resulted in significant negative effect on the team. When team members saw bickering and dissension between the formal and informal leader, it influenced how team members felt about leadership and the organization as a whole. Participants confirmed feelings of confusion related to what was going on with the two leaders, and began to perceive the formal leader negatively, especially if the informal leader was more positive.

When the informal leader was negative in interacting with the formal leader and other team members, and the formal leader did nothing to stop the negative behavior, team members perceived that the formal leader was lacking in leadership competencies and strength. Such situations resulted in the overall distrust of the formal leader. The interactions with a positive formal leader and a negative informal leader resulted in distrust of the informal leader and more connection to the formal leader. However, if the formal leader did not reel in the negativity, team members began to lose respect for the formal leader. Some participants reported that in such situations, employees felt that they had no protection against the tactics of the negative informal leader. This paradigm undermines the psychological expectations of the social workplace contract and will result in weakened organizational identity and enhanced employee disengagement.

If both the formal and informal leader were perceived as negative, team members witnessed existent power struggles between the two. Participants supported that such interactions not only made the work difficult but it also made the environment tense and uncomfortable for everyone. Team members would spend unproductive time talking about the tense relationship and other difficulties observed between the two. The situation was deemed a distraction and undermined individual and team productivity. The one positive aspect of this level of negative interaction was that some participants stated that the tension at the top caused some team members to forge closer work relationships among team members to protect each other and get the work accomplished.

Although a negative informal leader did not directly influence individual employee work behaviors, in times of major change this informal leader had some level of influence at the individual level. When the formal and informal leaders had discord, if a change initiative was introduced that was unpopular, team members tended to engage more with a negative informal leader's posture against the change. Despite the distrust or dislike of the negative informal leader, team members would unite with the informal leader in resistance to change or change initiatives. This is likely due to the fact that the informal leader was more vocal and perceived as more likely to say what other team members might not be willing to say.

Informal Leader and OCBs

Germinal organizational citizenship behaviors (OCBs) research supports that leaders who employ self-promoting behaviors are generally perceived as negative leaders and as a result encouraged less trust and less employee loyalty than leaders who exhibited self-sacrificial behaviors (Arnold & Loughlin, 2010; McKenna & Brown, 2011). Although individuals were not necessarily prone to follow this informal leader's lead, participants supported that such negativity by a strong informal leader made it easier for individuals who were also negative to exhibit more anti-social behaviors. Past research findings confirm that employees expect leaders to manage issues that arise in the team to include proficiently resolving conflict in the team environment. When such did not occur, the current study revealed that leadership actions directly influence team OCBs.

Study participants suggested that when the formal leader did not understand or ignored the influence of informal leaders, especially if negative, team productivity and team member motivation were decreased. The study results suggested that formal leaders must be cognizant of the informal leader's effect on team OCBs, team members' responses, and team member morale. When formal leaders understand how the informal leader might be able to influence team OCBs, formal leaders may be better equipped to galvanize team members support and engagement.

Positive Informal Leader and OCB Impact

Positive informal leaders were influential in all aspects of team OCBs and inclined to promote these behaviors despite existing negative conditions. These informal leaders exhibited a strong foundation of authentic leadership. They maximally encouraged altruism in the team dynamic, consistently encouraging team members to communicate openly and share information freely. They were courteous to all team members, even when frustrated by existing conditions, they were known to suppress their personal desires for the good of the team. These are the prevailing tenants of authentic leadership.

Although the conscientiousness construct is driven by intrinsic character traits, these leaders were perceived to have some influence on workplace conscientiousness and individual work efforts. They were considered to be very conscientious themselves and very focused on getting assigned tasks completed with as much proficiency as the work environment would allow. As a result, the majority of participants reported that these leaders directly influenced their work behaviors in that they were more conscientious in assuring a degree of excellence in their work output as well.

The positive informal leaders were strong proponents of team members showing sportsmanship behavior among team members, not only resisting the urge to complain but also often refusing to entertain hearing others criticize or complain. They were strongly civic minded, consistently encouraging team members to work diligently to help each other and work together to achieve set goals. In order to obtain maximum productivity from team members, formal leaders must be able to inspire trust and tap into team member OCBs. Building a positive relationship with the positive informal leader will aid in the formal leader's capacity to maximize team OCBs.

Negative Informal Leader and OCB Impact

Although the negative informal leader did not influence individual employee performance and work output, these leaders did impact team OCBs in the workplace significantly. The negative leader's influence did not completely stop a change initiative. However, progress in some initiatives was somewhat hindered due to the negative informal leader's influence through dominant coalitions. Participants indicated that this leader made it difficult for teams to develop OCBs in the team dynamic. Negative informal leaders were most influential as it related to altruism, courtesy, sportsmanship, and civic virtue and less influential on conscientiousness. In all instances, the influence of the negative informal leader resulted in hindering team OCBs.

The negative informal leader countered altruism in that team members perceived that the informal leader purposely made collaboration, communication, and task completions more difficult. These leaders were rarely courteous, kind, or optimistic and rarely promoted others to be likewise. Team members perceived that the informal leader encouraged unsportsmanship behaviors by exhibiting bad attitudes about the leader and the organization and, thus, promoted a climate of complaining and decreased motivation.

When dealing with a negative informal leader, civic virtue was absent as participants consistently supported that team members adopted attitudes of disengagement and hopelessness because of the interactions. The only aspect of OCBs in which the negative informal leader did not have a strong influence on was conscientiousness. Although they made it difficult for team members to accomplish tasks as a team, these leaders did not completely undermine a team member's work ethic in doing their job with proficiency.

Formal Leader Trust on OCBs

As participants provided feedback on their perspectives of informal leadership influence on the team dynamic, participants suggested that the formal leader's character and level of trust might have more importance on team OCBs than the character of the informal leader. The findings in the study aligned with the social exchange theory which states that when employees perceived that the formal leader was trustworthy and just, employees were willing to go above and beyond to achieve goals. Participants supported that when team members perceived that the formal leader was not concerned with the team member's best interest, team members had no trust in leadership and team OCBs were hindered.

Research supports that employee confidence in and willingness to trust organizational leadership is waning, with a perception that senior leaders look out only for themselves. With several formal leaders being perceived as negative, participants reported that the negative interactions of the formal leader negatively influenced team member's capacity to trust. As a result, there was less effort to exhibit OCBs.

Team Cohesion and Team OCBs

Outcomes of this study support that the informal leader had significant influence on how teams collaborated to achieve organizational goals. Team cohesion and collaboration were directly influenced by four of the five OCB dimensions: altruism, courtesy, conscientiousness, and sportsmanship. This study did not support that civic virtue was generally influenced by the cohesiveness within the team dynamic.

In the current study, team members were reportedly more apt to exhibit altruistic behaviors with each other when a foundation of trust has been laid within the team. The positive informal leader played a significant role in laying that foundation. This leader encouraged collaboration and sharing, while the negative informal leader discouraged the construct. Team members were likely to exhibit courtesy if they perceive that being kind and courteous would not be perceived as a weakness in the team and no one would take advantage of the team member. The informal leaders, positive and negative, influenced how this construct was perceived.

Team member conscientiousness was influenced by how much team members trusted each other to be supportive of each other in completing tasks. Team members perceived that the positive informal leader ensured that team members focused on coming together to successfully complete the assigned task rather than on how team members felt about the task. The negative informal leader was perceived as purposely undermining successful task achievement.

Feedback from the study supported that the informal leader's interaction with team members at all levels directly influenced the sportsmanship construct. The positive informal leader infused a foundation for team members to believe that what they did as a team mattered. This encouraged more unified team actions. The negative informal leader had the capacity to tear teams down and cause friction in the team dynamics. This resulted in team division and, in some instances, interpersonal team member conflict. The negative informal leaders negatively influenced the overall team culture.

Informal Leader and Team Cohesion

Effective teams must be able to maximize the knowledge and expertise of team members for organizational proficiency. Formal leaders should understand the dynamics of developing team cognition to promote maximum productivity in the team dynamic. Study participants' feedback supported that when formal leaders were not aware of the needs of team members, team collaboration was challenged. Such situations resulted in team members embracing the belief that the formal leaders did not care or appreciate the team members' contributions. When team members began to lose confidence that the formal leader valued employee service, study outcomes supported that team members lost the desire to engage in the formal leader's goals. This resulted in team members having no desire to exhibit citizenship or pro-social behaviors in the team dynamic.

Participants of the study collectively agreed that the informal leader has a strong influence on the team's mental models. In assessing how the informal leader influenced team mental modeling, team cohesion emerged as one of the strongest areas in which the informal leader wields a significant level of influence. Participants almost unanimously agreed that the informal leader had the potential to unify or divide team members.

The Positive Influence

Study participants conclusively agreed that positive informal leaders actively promoted team effectiveness and synergy, which undergirded team cognition. They purported that this leader was a team player who emphasized cohesiveness to achieve organizational goals. They were perceived as a team member who always had the work group's best interest at heart and wanted what was best for team members. They promoted sharing of knowledge and ideas, which rubbed off on everyone. Their positive attitude to get things done made team members want to align with leadership directives do what was needed to get it done. This informal leader's attitude of engagement was deemed the key to them being identified as an informal leader within the team.

Because of the way this leader made team members feel, they were generally the one that team member talked to concerning team issues or concerns. They were considered a key to communication and information flow within the team and with the formal leader. Participants identified this leader as the glue that held the team together. Because this leader was generally immune to what was termed "the mess", their opinion was highly valued and team members readily sought them out for advice and counsel. They helped promote open dialogue and were trusted to present the ideas of the team to the formal leader to ensure ideas were considered and issues were addressed. The informal leader's capacity to communicate in a positive way prompted team members to be more open in communication with formal authority as well.

The positive informal leader was also deemed instrumental in promoting team spirit in the team dynamic. They were perceived as embracing of varying team member ideas and never judgmental. They did not want to promote an environment where people were uncomfortable coming to work. As a result, other team members likewise engaged to make the work environment a comfortable one. Because this leader generally held referent power, they encouraged team members to fully embrace formal leader authority.

The Negative Influence

Informal leaders who were identified as negative undermined team cohesion. Participants agreed that although the negative informal leader had the potential to bring team members together, they seem to purposely choose to tear down. They promoted a non-sharing, non-collaborative culture. Their influence produced negative outcomes even when the informal leader seemingly sought to do something positive.

In order to get things done, these leaders often used scare tactics and were often deemed deceptive. They were inclined to be negatively self-governing, often ignoring team norms and organizational rules to do what they desired. Much of their base of authority was due to their longevity in the organization, which undergirds their influence in being able to mobilize support for their ideas. Participants relayed that often these individuals presented information to the team in a way that made team members feel as if they had been misled. They had a tendency to seek to undermine team trust among team members and hinder team collaboration. When such interactions were allowed to continue, team members saw the disruption as a direct reflection on the formal leader. Team member had an expectation that the formal leader would take a stand of authority to stop the informal leader's negative posturing. Failure of such expectations caused team members to doubt the formal leader's authority and reduced respect in the formal leader. A number of participants stated in some instances they believed the formal leader feared the informal leader, especially if the informal leader had longevity and was connected to perceived dominant coalitions.

Team Member Engagement

The current study supports that the most significant factor in promoting team engagement in the team environment was the relationship and interactions between the formal and informal leaders. Fifty percent of participants specifically used the term *positive interactions* to define the most influential aspect of team engagement. When the relationship between the formal and positive informal leaders was deemed positive, the two seemed to work well together, promoting more team unity. Team members appreciated seeing the two bounced off each other. In task accomplishment, team members tended to be more responsive to doing what the formal leader asked. Positive interactions promoted more team orientation.

Study participants stated that positive interactions led to more pro-social behaviors. Team members felt confident that they could do more and be successful at the tasks that were given. They felt encouraged by the positive team culture and wanted to get more involved. They further suggested that the positive team culture infused a team spirit of open communication, sharing, and learning from one another. The more positive the interaction between a respective positive informal leader and formal leader, the more the team engaged with the leadership and the organization. Participants added that if interactions became negative, team engagement diminished likewise.

Informal Leader and Corporate Culture

Organizational culture is the composite of shared mental assumptions among team members that guide actions, behaviors, and responses based on past perceptual outcomes. Although creation of the overall corporate culture was not directly connected to the informal leader, there was a connection to specific team cultures. At the onset of the study, organizational culture was not included as a component of the study focus. However, by the third interview, organizational culture began to emerge as a consistent theme in informal leadership influence and team engagement. In keeping consistency in the interview protocol, none of the additional participants was asked about culture. Even though it was not among the questions presented to participants, 80% of participants introduced "culture" as having influence on how team members perceived organizational leadership.

Participants assessed that the capacity of team members to be productive in a cultural paradigm was influenced by several factors. The lack of accessibility to the formal leader was one factor that was suggested that made team members feel alienated and unimportant. The lack of collaboration and sharing was also directly linked to culture. The negativity of the culture tended to promote feelings of being overwhelmed, overworked, and unappreciated with no one to speak for team members or fight for what team members needed or desired. Participants supported that when leaders failed to provide what employees needed on the job (social workplace contract), team members felt no obligation to invest in or exhibit pro-social behaviors, which tended to promote more cultural negativity.

The majority of study participants suggested that if formal leaders were cognizant of how the culture hindered positive interactions, they would have been more focused on minimizing negativity within the culture and changes would be magnified with more proficiency. The more negative the perceived culture, the less pro-social behaviors were exhibited from team members.

Culture and Engagement

In the current study, the negative informal leader was directly correlated to the existence of a negative culture and purportedly used the negativity of the culture to promote their own agendas. Participants introduced the construct of culture as a problem in the organizational paradigm, describing a non-constructive culture. Team collaborations and team unity were deemed difficult to achieve because of a culture that promoted discord and divisiveness.

Of those who referenced culture, most defined traits that aligned with the aggressive-defensive or passive-defensive culture. In these cultures, team members were generally angry, mistreated each other, and were disengaged. Participants supported that the main source of information was through the grapevine with the informal leader being the carrier of most of the news. Most employees felt it was difficult to assess what was true and what was not because very little communication came from formal communication channels.

The negativity within the culture did not promote positive attitudes or actions among team members, even if a positive informal leader tried to encourage positivity. Team members were inclined to focus on taking care of self, rather than emotionally investing in the organization. Participants affirmed that many team members adopted a "if they don't bother me, I don't bother them" mentality, or "I'm just here to do my job, get my paycheck, and go home". Employees perceived that nobody in leadership cared about them or what they were enduring in the culture. As a result, employees were prone to do just enough to keep their jobs with no real engagement to the organizational mission.

When the formal leader was new to the team, most of the team tended to minimize interactions with the new leader because of a lack of trust in anyone in a leadership position. New leader had to prove they were trust-worthy. In such cultures, leader-member exchange (LMX) was considered low quality with disengagement being the norm. These low-quality LMX interactions negatively influence how team members perceive each other, the leader, and the organization.

Corporate Culture Influence on Team OCBs

An organization's culture generally ranges from very weak to very strong, dependent upon the degree of influence it has on team members. A culture is considered strong when behaviors of team members are consistent based on known expectations, consequences, and outcomes. A culture is considered negative when the expected outcomes promote negative team member behaviors and actions. Study participants consistently supported the negativity in the culture was strong and deeply ingrained in organizational operations.

The positive informal leader perceptually had the capacity to minimize some of the negative effects of the negative culture on team OCBs but not reverse the negative effects. The negative culture undermined altruism as team members did not perceive an advantage of open communication and collaboration. Team members were not prone to exhibit courtesy in the team dynamic because the negativity of the culture provided excuses for negative attitudes.

In a negative culture, team members who were generally conscientious as a personality trait were often persuaded to minimize their work efforts for fear of infringing on other people's territory or being perceived as competitive. Sportsmanship and civic virtue were minimized because team members did not perceive that the organization was concerned about the best interest of employees. As such, team members neither were predisposed to positive affirmations of the workplace nor were willing to risk opening themselves up to hope only to be disappointed. In an aggressive or passive defensive culture, members are less likely to promote high-quality service but focus more on ensuring that policies are followed at all costs often to the detriment of organizational success in the marketplace.

In the few instances in which employees perceived a positive work culture, participants supported that they felt that their actions were readily acknowledged and rewarded. As a result, they felt that they were valued and their efforts appreciated. This encouraged more willingness to exhibit OCBs. Employees in positive cultures were more prone to adapt and readily embrace change and transitions. The positive culture directly influenced employee's work behaviors, attitudes, and service delivery mentality.

To lay a strong foundation for a positive team culture (constructive culture) that readily embraces change initiatives, formal leaders should continuously monitor organizational and team interactions for signs that could lead to high levels of disengaged team members. Leaders might be equally vigilant in monitoring the actions and behaviors of informal leaders to deter negative posturing. The goal of the empowered leader must be to build a foundation for a strong, positive culture to maximize organizational success, especially related to change.

Conclusion

I have worked in human resource management for more than 30 years as an HR employee, manager, and consultant. I've worked in and with diverse industries to include educational entities, medical practices, corporations, federal agencies, state government, city municipalities, and non-profits. Many organizations in today's global work environment still operate as a hierarchical (governed by rules, policies, and strict structures), passive-aggressive work culture in which employees align with expectations to ensure job security. This cultural mix is a recipe for an unhappy, demotivated, and disengaged workforce in which change will likely not be embraced with excitement.

The good news for most organizations is that even in the midst of hierarchical, passive-aggressive cultures, managerial leaders indicate a strong desire for employees to feel connected to the organization and its mission. Most leaders express a verbal desire for their employees to feel valued and appreciated. Furthermore, they affirm that they realize employees are the most valuable asset to the organization. Although some organizations, like the military, still must employ a more regimented structure, most mainstream organizational leader express a desire for a more engaging work environment, such as a clan based, constructive work culture, which is the cultural paradigm needed for a fully engaged workforce.

With the high failure rate of change initiatives, empowered leaders must be cognizant of every strategy available to maximize change successes. In assessing the role of an informal leader in helping formal leaders achieve success in change initiatives, study participants confirmed that informal leaders influence the interpersonal interactions at all levels of organizational operations. Understanding the implications of the study as it relates to the informal leader behaviors, formal leader trust, citizenship behaviors, team cohesion, and corporate culture can provide invaluable information to help formal organizational leadership maximize support for organizational change initiatives.

Positive informal leaders, properly managed and engaged in the team composite, can help formal leaders create the positive culture that is desired to fully engage team members. Empowered formal leaders must be constantly aware of what is going on within the team dynamic in order to strategize the most effective way to engage staff to align with what's needed for organizational success. Positive informal leaders can be the linchpin in helping empowered leaders lay a strong foundation to maximize employee engagement to achieve a leader's desired change initiative and ensure long-term organizational success.

Bibliography

Ahmad, A., & Omar, Z. (2013). Abusive supervision and deviant workplace behavior: The mediating role of work-family conflict. *The Journal of Human Resource and Adult Learning, 9*(2), 124–130.

Anderson, C. (2010). Presenting and valuating qualitative research. *American Journal of Pharmaceutical Education, 74*(8), Article 141, 1–7.

Arnold, K., & Loughlin, C. (2010). Individually considerate transformational leadership behavior and self-sacrifice. *Leadership & Organization Development Journal, 31*(8), 670–686. doi:10.1108/01437731011094748

Arthur, C., & Hardy, L. (2014). Transformational leadership: A quasi-experimental study. *Leadership & Organization Development Journal, 35*(1), 38–53. doi:10.1108/LODJ-03-2012-0033

ASHE. (2006). Empowered leaders everywhere: The democratic distribution of power. *ASHE Higher Education Report, 31*(6), 79–81.

Ashforth, B., Harrison, S., & Corley, K. (2008). Identification in organizations: An examination of four fundamental questions. *Journal of Management, 34*(3), 325–374.

Autry, A. (2019). 2018 employee engagement & loyalty statistics. *Access Perks*. Retrieved from https://blog.accessperks.com/2018-employee-engagement-loyalty-statistics#1

Badshah, S. (2012). Historical study of leadership theories. *Journal of Strategic Human Resource Management, 1*(1), 49–59.

Bak, O. (2011). The role of qualitative research in a mixed methods study: Assessing the e-business enabled transformation in a strategic business unit. *Qualitative Research Journal, 11*(2) 76–84. doi:10.3316/QRJ1102076

Bankar, S., & Gankar, S. (2013). Employee engagement and change management. *Journal of Commerce & Management Thought IV, 2*, 313–321.

Bârgau, M. (2015). Leadership versus management. *Romanian Economic and Business Review, 10*(2), 197–204.

Barth, R. (2002). The culture builder. *Educational Leadership, 59*(8), 6–11.

Bass, B. (2008). *Bass & Stogdill's handbook of leadership: Theory, research, & managerial applications* (4th ed.). New York City: Free Press.

Bathurst, R., & Monin, N. (2010). Shaping leadership for today: Mary Parker Follettt's aesthetic. *Leadership, 6*(2), 115–131. doi:10.1177/1742715010363206

Batool, S. (2013). Developing organizational commitment and organizational justice to amplify organizational citizenship behavior in banking sector. *Pakistan Journal of Commerce and Social Sciences, 7*(3), 646–655.

Battilana, J., Gilmartin, M., Sengul, M., Pache, A., & Alexander, J. (2010). Leadership competencies for implementing planned organizational change. *The Leadership Quarterly, 21*(3), 422–438. doi:10.1016/j.leaqua.2010.03.007

Beheshtifar, M., & Hesani, G. (2013). Organizational citizenship behavior (OCB): A factor to decrease organizational conflict. *Interdisciplinary Journal of Contemporary Research in Business, 5*(1), 214–222.

Belogolovsky, E., & Somech, A. (2010). Teachers' organizational citizenship behavior: Examining the boundary between in-role behavior and extra-role behavior from the perspective of teachers, principals and parents. *Teaching and Teacher Education, 26*(4), 914–923. doi:10.1016/j.tate.2009.10.032

Beranek, P., & Clairborne, M. (2012). The impact of training on virtual project teams: A TIP investigation. *International Journal of Information Technology Project Management (IJITPM), 3*(1), 36–48. doi:10.4018/jitpm.2012010103

Berry, C., Ones, D., & Sackett, P. (2007). Interpersonal deviance, organizational deviance, and their common correlates: A review and meta-analysis. *Journal of Applied Psychology, 92*, 410–424.

Beverland, M., & Lindgreen, A. (2010). What makes a good case study? A positivist review of qualitative case research published in industrial marketing management, 1971–2006. *Industrial Marketing Management, 39*(1), 56–63.

Bhuvanaiah, T., & Raya, R. (2014). Employee engagement: Key to organizational success. *SCMS Journal of Indian Management, 11*(4), 61–71.

Bligh, M., Kohles, J., & Pillai, R. (2011). Romancing leadership: Past, present, and future. *The Leadership Quarterly, 22*, 1058–1077. doi:10.1016/j.leaqua.2011.09.003

Boje, D., & Rosile, G. (2001). Where's the power in empowerment? Answers from Follettt and Clegg'. *Journal of Applied Behavioral Science, 37*(1), 90–117.

Bonebright, D. (2010). 40 years of storming: A historical review of Tuckman's model of small group development. *Human Resource Development International, 13*(1), 111–120.

Bouckenooghe, D. (2010). Positioning change recipients' attitudes toward change in the organizational change literature. *The Journal of Applied Behavioral Science, 46*, 500–531. doi: 10.1177/0021886310367944

Bringselius, L. (2014). Employee objections to organizational change: A framework for addressing management responses. *Organization Development Journal, 32*(1), 41–54.

Brisson-Banks, C. (2010). Managing change and transitions: A comparison of different models and their commonalities. *Library Management, 31*(4/5), 241–252. doi:10.1108/01435121011046317

Buchbinder, E. (2011). Beyond checking: Experiences of the validation interview. *Qualitative Social Work, 10*(1), 106–122.

Buljac, M., Van Woerkom, M., Van Wijngaarden, J., & Ananthaswamy, M. (2013). Are real teams healthy teams? *Journal of Healthcare Management, 58*(2), 92–109.

Busse, R. (2014). Comprehensive leadership review–literature, theories, and research. *Advances in Management, 7*(5), 52–66.

By, R. (2005). Organisational change management: A critical review. *Journal of Change Management, 5*(4), 369–380.

Carillo, K., & Okoli, C. (2011). Generating quality open content: A functional group perspective based on the time, interaction, and performance theory. *Information & Management, 48*(6), 208–219. doi:10.1016/j.im.2011.04.004

Casey, D., & Houghton, C. (2010). Clarifying case study research: Examples from practice. *Nurse Researcher, 17*(3), 41–51.

Cavazotte, F., Moreno, V., & Hickmann, M. (2012). Effects of leader intelligence, personality and emotional intelligence on transformational leadership and managerial performance. *The Leadership Quarterly, 23*, 443–455. doi:10.1016/j.leaqua.2011.10.003

Cherniss, C. (2010). Emotional intelligence: New insights and further clarifications. *Industrial & Organizational Psychology, 3*(2), 183–191.

Cho, Y., & Park, H. (2011). Exploring the relationships among trust, employee satisfaction, and organizational commitment. *Public Management Review, 13*(4), 551–573. doi:10.1080/14719037.2010.525033

Choi, J., & Sy, T. (2010). Group-level organizational citizenship behavior: Effects of demographic faultlines and conflict in small work groups. *Journal of Organizational Behavior, 31*, 1032–1054. doi:10.1002/job.661

Chung, C. (2013). The road not taken: Putting "management" back to Taylor's scientific management. *Journal of Multidisciplinary Research, 5*(1), 45–56.

Cianci, A., Hannah, S., Roberts, R., & Tsakumis, G. (2014). The effects of authentic leadership on followers' ethical decision-making in the face of temptation: An experimental study. *The Leadership Quarterly, 25*, 581–594. doi:10.1016/j.leaqua.2013.12.001

Cooke, N., Gorman, J., Myers, C., & Duran, J. (2013). Interactive team cognition. *Cognitive Science, 37*(2), 255–285. doi:10.1111/cogs.12009

Cooper, K., & White, R. (2012). *Qualitative research in the post-modern era, contexts of qualitative research.* New York, NY: Springer Publishing. doi:10.1007/978-94-007-2339-9

Côté, S., Lopes, P., Salovey, P., & Miners, C. (2010). Emotional intelligence and leadership emergence in small groups. *The Leadership Quarterly, 21*(3), 496–508. doi:10.1016/j.leaqua.2010.03.012

Creswell, J. (2013). *Qualitative inquiry and research design: Choosing among five approaches* (3rd ed.). Thousand Oaks, CA: Sage Publications.

Crossman, B., & Crossman, J. (2011). Conceptualising followership: A review of the literature. *Leadership, 7*, 481–497. doi:10.1177/1742715011416891

Crowe, S., Cresswell, K., Robertson, A., Huby, G., Avery, A., & Shiekh, A. (2011). The case study approach. *BMC Medical Research Methodology, 11*(100), 1–9. doi:10.1186/1471-2288-11-100

Cunliffe, A., & Eriksen, M. (2011). Relational leadership. *Human Relations, 64*(11), 1425–1449. doi:10.1177/0018726711418388

Cunningham, J., Salomone, J., & Wielgus, N. (2015). Project management leadership style: A team member perspective. *International Journal of Global Business, 8*(2), 27–54.

DeChurch, L., & Mesmer-Magnus, J. (2010). Measuring shared team mental models: A meta-analysis. *Group Dynamics: Theory, Research, and Practice, 14*(1), 1–14. doi:10.1037/a0017455

DeConinck, J. (2010). The effect of organizational justice, perceived organizational support, and perceived supervisor support on marketing employees' level of trust. *Journal of Business Research, 63*(12), 1349–1355. doi:10.1016/j.jbusres.2010. 01.003

Denzin, N. (2012). Triangulation 2.0. *Journal of Mixed Methods Research, 6*(2), 80–88. doi:10.1177/1558689812437186

DeOrtentiis, P., Summers, J., Ammeter, A., Douglas, C., & Ferris, G. (2013). Cohesion and satisfaction as mediators of the team trust–team effectiveness relationship: An interdependence theory perspective. *Career Development International, 18*(5), 521–543. doi:10.1108/CDI-03-2013-0035

Dimitrov, K. (2013). Edgar Schein's model of organizational culture levels as a hologram. *Economic Studies, 22*(4), 3–36.

Downey, M., Parslow, S., & Smart, M. (2011). The hidden treasure in nursing leadership: Informal leaders. *Journal of Nursing Management, 19*(4), 517–521. doi:1 0.1111/j.1365-2834.2011.01253

Du, J., & Choi, J. (2013). Leadership effectiveness in China: The moderating role of change climate. *Social Behavior and Personality, 41*(9), 1571–1583. doi:10.2224/ sbp.2013.41.9.1571

Easton, G. (2010). Critical realism in case study research. *Industrial Marketing Management, 39*(1), 118–128.

Follett Parker, M. (1918). *The new state.* Chapter 14: The group principle at work. Retrieved September 5, 2010, from http://sunsite.utk.edu/FINS/Mary_Parker_ Follettt/XIV.txt

Forsyth, D. (2006). *Group dynamics* (5th ed.). Belmont, CA: Wadsworth Cengage Learning.

French, J., Jr., & Raven, B. (1959). The bases of social power. *Studies in Social Power (Institute for Social Research, Ann Arbor, MI)*, 150–167.

Fuchs, S., & Edwards, M. (2012). Predicting pro-change behaviour: The role of perceived organisational justice and organisational identification. *Human Resource Management Journal, 22*(1), 39–59.

Gijselaers, W., Woltjer, G., Segers, M., van den Bossche, P., & Kirschner, P. (2011). Team learning: Building shared mental models. *Instructional Science, 39*(3), 283–301. doi:10.1007/s11251-010-9128-3

Gilley, A., & Kerno, S. (2010). Groups, teams, and communities of practice: A comparison. *Advances in Developing Human Resources, 12*(1), 46–60. doi:10. 1177/1523422310365312

Gitman, L. et al. (2018). *Introduction to business.* Houston, TX: OpenStax Rice University.

Gläser, J., & Laudel, G. (2013). Life with and without coding: Two methods for early-stage data analysis in qualitative research aiming at causal explanations. *Forum: Qualitative Social Research, 14*(2), 1–38.

Goleman, D. (1998). What makes a leader? *Harvard Business Review, 76*(6), 93–102.

Gordon, J. (2018). *The power of a positive team.* Hoboken, NJ: Wiley & Sons.

Halevy, N., Berson, Y., & Galinsky, A. (2011). The mainstream is not electable: When vision triumphs over representativeness in leader emergence and effectiveness. *Personality & Social Psychology, 37*(7), 893–904. doi:10.1177/0146167211402836

Han, G., & Harms, P. (2010). Team identification, trust and conflict: A mediation model. *International Journal of Conflict Management, 21*(1), 20–43. doi:10.1108/10444061011016614

Hansen, A., Byrne, Z., & Kiersch, C. (2014). How interpersonal leadership relates to employee engagement. *Journal of Managerial Psychology, 29*(8), 953–972. doi:10.1108/JMP-11-2012-0343

Hare, A. (2010). Theories of group development and categories for interaction analysis. *Small Group Research, 41*(1), 106–140. doi:10.1177/1046496409359503

Harun, S., Soran, S., & Caymaz, E. (2014). Dark side of Organizational Citizenship Behavior (OCB): Testing a model between OCB, social loafing, and organizational commitment. *International Journal of Business and Social Science, 5*(5), 125–135.

Hashim, M. (2013). Change management. *International Journal of Academic Research in Business and Social Sciences, 3*(7), 685–694. doi:10.6007/IJARBSS/v3-i7/92

Hassard, J. (2012). Rethinking the Hawthorne Studies: The Western Electric research in its social, political and historical context. *Human Relations, 65*(1), 1431–1461. doi:10.1177/0018726712452168

Hechanova, R., & Cementina-Olpoc, R. (2013). Transformational leadership, change management, and commitment to change: A comparison of academic and business organizations. *The Asia-Pacific Education Researcher, 22*(1), 11–19. doi:10.1007/s40299-012-0019

Hernandez, M., Eberly, M., Avolio, B., & Johnson, M. (2011). The loci and mechanisms of leadership: Exploring a more comprehensive view of leadership theory. *The Leadership Quarterly, 22*(6), 1165–1185. doi:10.1016/j.leaqua.2011.09.009

Ho, J., Poeta, D., Jacobson, T., Zolnik, T., Neske, G., Connors, B., & Burwell, R. (2015). Bidirectional modulation of recognition memory. *The Journal of Neuroscience, 35*(39), 23–35. doi:10.1523/JNEUROSCI.2278-15.2015

Hoe, J., & Hoare, Z. (2012). Understanding quantitative research: Part 1. *Learning Zone: Continuing Professional Development, 27*(15–17), 52–57.

Houghton, C., Casey, D., Shaw, D., & Murphy, K. (2013). Rigour in qualitative case-study research. *Nurse Researcher, 20*(4), 12–17.

Hui, C., Lam, S., & Law, K. (2000). Instrumental values of organizational citizenship behavior for promotion: A field quasi-experiment. *Journal of Applied Psychology, 85*(5), 822–828.

Jacobs, S., Rouse, P., & Parsons, M. (2014). Leading change within health services. *Leadership in Health Services, 27*(2), 72–86. doi.org/10.1108/LHS-10-2012-0033

Javadi, M., & Ahmadi, A. (2013). Investigating the roles of organizational culture, leadership style, and employee engagement in knowledge transfer. *International Journal of Academic Research in Business and Social Sciences, 3*(9), 717–734.

Jha, S., & Jha, S. (2013). Leader-member exchange: A critique of theory & practice. *Journal of Management and Public Policy, 4*(2), 42–54.

Jiao, C., Richards, D., & Zhang, K. (2011). Leadership and organizational citizenship behavior: OCB-specific meanings as mediators. *Journal of Business and Psychology, 26*(1), 11–25.

Jick, T. (1995). Accelerating change for competitive advantage. *Organizational Dynamics, 24*(1), 77–82.

Johnson, M., Hollenbeck, J., Scott, D., Barnes, C., & Jundt, D. (2013). Functional versus dysfunctional team change: Problem diagnosis and structural feedback for self-managed teams. *Organizational Behavior and Human Decision Processes, 122*(1), 1–11. doi:10.1016/j.obhdp.2013.03.006

Johnson, R., & Jackson, E. (2012). When opposites do (and do not) attract: Interplay of leader and follower self-identities and its consequences for leader-member exchange. *The Leadership Quarterly, 23*(3), 488–501. doi:10.1016/j.leaqua.2011.12.003

Kahn, W. (1990). Psychological conditions of personal engagement and disengagement at work. *The Academy of Management Journal, 33*(4), 692–724. doi:10.2307/256287

Kanihan, S., Hansen, K., Blair, S., Shore, M., & Myers, J. (2013). Communication managers in the dominant coalition. *Journal of Communication Management, 17*(2), 140–156. doi:10.1108/13632541311318747

Kanwal, I., Lodhi, R., & Kashif, M. (2019). Leadership styles and workplace ostracism among frontline employees. *Management Research Review, 42*(8), 991–1013.

Kapoulas, A., & Mitic, M. (2012). Understanding challenges of qualitative research: Rhetorical issues and reality traps. *Qualitative Market Research: An International Journal, 15*(4), 1352–2752. doi:10.1108/13522751211257051

Katz, R. (1955). Skills of an effective administrator. *Harvard Business Review, 33*(1), 33–42.

Khan, Z., & Katzenbach, J. (2007). Peak performance. *Leadership Excellence, 24*(10), 10.

Kim, H. (2014). Transformational leadership, organizational clan culture, organizational affective commitment, and organizational citizenship behavior: A case of South Korea's public sector. *Public Organization Review, 14*(3), 397–417. doi.org/10.1007/s11115-013-0225-z

Kim, J., & Mondello, M. (2014). Structural examination of managerial work values and constructive organizational culture: Use of the partial disaggregation method. *Journal of Multidisciplinary Research, 6*(2), 5–14.

King, E., George, J., & Hebl, M. (2005). Linking personality to helping behaviors at work: An interactional perspective. *Journal of Personality, 73*, 585–607.

Kirmani, S., Attiq, S., Bakari, H., & Irfan, M. (2019). Role of core self evaluation and acquired motivations in employee task performance. *Pakistan Journal of Psychological Research, 34*(2), 401–418. doi:10.33824/PJPR.2019.34.2.22

Klein, A. (2011). Corporate culture: Its value as a resource for competitive advantage. *Journal of Business Strategy, 32*(2), 21–28. doi.org/10.1108/02756661111109743

Kopelman, R., Prottas, D., & Davis, A. (2008). Douglas McGregor's theory X and Y: Toward a construct-valid measure. *Journal of Managerial Issues, 20*, 255–271.

Kotter, J. (1990a). What leaders really do. *Harvard Business Review, 68*, 103–111.

Kotter, J. (1990b). *A force for change: How leadership differs from management.* New York, NY: Free Press.

Kotter, J. (1995). Leading change: Why transformation efforts fail. *Harvard Business Review, 73*(2), 59–67.

Kotter, J. (2001). What leaders really do? *Harvard Business Review, 79*(11), 85–96.

Kotter, J., & Schlesinger, L. (2008). Choosing strategies for change. *Harvard Business Review, 86*(7), 130–139.

Kotterman, J. (2006). Leadership vs management: What's the difference? *Journal for Quality & Participation, 29*(2), 13–17.

Kozlowski, S., & Chao, G. (2012). The dynamics of emergence: Cognition and cohesion in work teams. *Managerial & Decision Economics, 33*(5/6), 335–354. doi:10.1002/mde.2552

Krueger, D. (2013). Informal leaders and cultural change. *American Nurse Today, 8*(8).

Kutcher, E. (2013). Employee engagement: A workplace issue for dental assistants. *Dental Assistant, 82*(3), 34–38.

Kuvaas, B., Buch, R., Dysvik, A., & Haerem, T. (2012). Economic and social leader–member exchange relationships and follower performance. *The Leadership Quarterly, 23*, 756–765. doi:10.1016/j.leaqua.2011.12.013

Lai, J., Lam, L., & Lam, S. (2013). Organizational citizenship behavior in work groups: A team cultural perspective. *Journal of Organizational Behavior, 34*(7), 1039–1056. doi:10.1002/job.1840

Landis, E., Hill, D., & Harvey, M. (2014). A synthesis of leadership theories and styles. *Journal of Management Policy and Practice, 15*(2), 97–100.

Law, K., Wang, H., & Hui, C. (2010). Currencies of exchange and global LMX: How they affect employee task performance and extra-role performance. *Asia Pacific Journal of Management, 27*(4), 625–646. doi:10.1007/s10490-009-9141-8

Lawler, A., & Sillitoe, J. (2010). Perspectives on instituting change management in large organisations. *Australian Universities' Review, 52*(2), 43–48.

Le Blanc, P., & González-Romá, V. (2012). A team level investigation of the relationship between Leader–Member Exchange (LMX) differentiation, and commitment and performance. *The Leadership Quarterly, 23*(3), 534–544. doi:10.1016/j.leaqua.2011.12.006

Leech, N., & Onwuegbuzie, A. (2011). Beyond constant comparison qualitative data analysis: Using NVivo. *School Psychology Quarterly, 26*(1), 70–84. doi:10.1037/a0022711

Levine, E. (2010). Emotion and power (as social influence): Their impact on organizational citizenship and counterproductive individual and organizational behavior. *Human Resource Management Review, 20*(1), 4–17. doi:10.1016/j.hrmr.2009.03.011

Lewin, B., Hlupic, V., & Walton, C. (2010). Emergent leadership. *Leadership Excellence, 27*(3), 17.

Lewin, K. (1951). *Field theory in social science.* New York, NY: Harper & Row.

Lin, C., & Peng, T. (2010). From organizational citizenship behaviour to team performance: The mediation of group cohesion and collective efficacy. *Management and Organization Review, 6*(1), 55–75. doi:10.1111/j.1740-8784.2009.00172.x

Lin, Y. (2004). Organizational identity and its implication on organization development. *Academy of Human Resource Development, Symposium 37–2*, 803–810.

Lincoln, Y., & Guba, E. (1985). *Naturalistic inquiry*. Newbury Park, CA: Sage Publishing.

Lunenburg, F. (2011). Leadership versus Management: A key distinction–at least in theory. *International Journal of Management, Business, and Administration, 14*(1), 1–4.

Luria, G., & Berson, Y. (2013). How do leadership motives affect informal and formal leadership emergence? *Journal of Organizational Behavior, 34*, 995–1015. doi:10.1002/job.1836

Mahembe, B., & Engelbrecht, A. (2013). The relationship between servant leadership, affective team commitment and team effectiveness. *SA Journal of Human Resource Management, 11*(1), 1–10.

Martinez, A., Kane, R., Ferris, G., & Brooks, C. (2012). Power in leader-follower work relationships. *Journal of Leadership & Organizational Studies, 19*(2), 142–151. doi:10.1177/1548051811433358

McCleskey, J. (2014). Emotional intelligence and leadership: A review of the progress, controversy, and criticism. *International Journal of Organizational Analysis, 22*(1), 76–93. doi.org/10.1108/IJOA-03-2012-0568

McGrath, J. (1991). Time, Interaction, and Performance (TIP): A theory of groups. *Small Group Research, 22*, 147–174.

McGrath, J., & Bates, B. (2017). *The little book of big management theories*. Harlow, England: Pearson Publishers.

McGregor, D. (1967). *The professional manager*. New York, NY: McGraw-Hill Publishing.

McKenna, R., & Brown, T. (2011). Does sacrificial leadership have to hurt? The realities of putting others first. *Organization Development Journal, 29*(3), 39–50.

Mero-Jaffe, I. (2011). "Is that what I said?" Interview transcript approval by participants: An aspect of ethics in qualitative research. *The International Journal of Qualitative Methods, 10*(3), 221–230.

Mihaela, V., & Bratianu, C. (2012). Organizational culture modeling. *Management & Marketing, 7*(2), 257–276.

Morita, P., & Burns, C. (2014). Trust tokens in team development. *Team Performance Management, 20*(1/2), 39–64. doi.org/10.1108/TPM-03-2013-0006

Moskowitz, G. (2005). *Social cognition: Understanding self and others*. New York, NY: Guilford Press.

Mouton, N., Just, S., & Gabrielsen, J. (2012). Creating organizational cultures: Re-conceptualizing the relations between rhetorical strategies and material practices. *Journal of Organizational Change Management, 25*(2), 315–331. doi:10.1108/09534811211213973

Mulnix, M., Cojanu, K., & Pettine, S. (2011). Critical role of the dominant coalition in higher education marketing strategy formulation. *Research in Higher Education Journal, 11*, 1–10.

Muo, I. (2013). Motivating & managing knowledge workers: Evidence from diverse industries & cultures. *Journal of Management and Sustainability, 3*(2), 119–131.

Nair, N., & Bhatnagar, D. (2011). Understanding workplace deviant behavior in nonprofit organizations. *Nonprofit Management and Leadership, 21*(3), 289–309. doi:10.1002/nml.20026

Nasomboon, B. (2014). The relationship among leadership commitment, organizational performance, and employee engagement. *International Business Research*, *7*(9), 77–90. doi:10.5539/ibr.v7n9p77

Nemeth, C., Personnaz, B., Personnaz, M., & Goncalo, J. (2004). The liberating role of conflict in group creativity: A study in two countries. *European Journal of Social Psychology*, *34*(4), 365–374.

Ng'ambi, D., & Bozalek, V. (2013). Leveraging informal leadership in higher education institutions: A case of diffusion of emerging technologies in a southern context. *British Journal of Educational Technology*, *44*(6), 940–950. doi:10.1111/bjet.12108

Nichols, T., & Erakovich, R. (2013). Authentic leadership and implicit theory: A normative form of leadership? *Leadership & Organization Development Journal*, *34*(2), 182–195. doi:10.1108/01437731311321931

Nolan, S. (2010). Workplace flexibility. *Strategic HR Review*, *9*(2). doi:10.1108/shr.2010.37209baa.001

Northouse, P. (2008). *Leadership: Theory and practice*. Los Angeles: Sage Publications.

Northouse, P. (2018). *Leadership: Theory and practice* (8th ed.). Los Angeles: Sage Publications.

O'Kane, C., & Cunningham, J. (2012). Leadership changes and approaches during company turnaround. *International Studies of Management and Organization*, *42*(4), 52–85. doi:10.2753/IMO0020-8825420403

Onwuegbuzie, A., Johnson, R., & Collins, K. (2011). Assessing legitimation in mixed research: A new framework. *Quality & Quantity*, *45*(6), 1253–1271.

Onwuegbuzie, A., Leech, N., & Collins, K. (2012). Qualitative analysis techniques for the review of the literature. *The Qualitative Report*, *17*(56), 1–28.

https://d.docs.live.net/44f8c6e020c4e884/Documents/Downloads/15044-4146-Ref Mismatch Report.docx - LStERROR_34O'Reilly, M. (2012). "Unsatisfactory saturation": A critical exploration of the notion of saturated sample sizes in qualitative research. *Qualitative Research*, *13*(2), 190–197. doi:10.1177/14687941 12446106

Organ, D. (1988). *Organizational citizenship behavior: The good soldier syndrome*. Lexington, MA: Lexington Books.

Pardo-del-Val, M., Martínez-Fuentes, C., & Roig-Dobón, S. (2012). Participative management and its influence on organizational change. *Management Decision*, *50*(10), 1843–1860. doi:10.1108/00251741211279639

Pearce, J. (2010). A structural analysis of dominant coalitions in small banks. *Journal of Management*, *21*(6), 1075–1095.

Pielstick, C. (2000). Formal vs. informal leading: A comparative analysis. *Journal of Leadership Studies*, *7*(3), 99–116.

Podsakoff, N., Blume, B., Whiting, S., & Podsakoff, P. (2009). Individual- and organizational-level consequences of organizational citizenship behaviors: A meta-analysis. *Journal of Applied Psychology*, *94*(1), 122–141.

Podsakoff, P., MacKenzie, S., Paine, J., & Bachrach, D. (2000). Organizational citizenship behaviors: A critical review of the theoretical and empirical literature and suggestions for future research. *Journal of Management*, *26*(3), 513–548.

Qamar, N. (2012). Job satisfaction and organizational commitment as antecedents of Organizational Citizenship Behavior (OCB). *Interdisciplinary Journal of Contemporary Research In Business, 4*(7), 103–122.

Qu, S., & Dumay, J. (2011). The qualitative research interview. *Qualitative Research in Accounting & Management, 8*(3), 238–264. doi:10.1108/11766091111162070

Ravasi, D., & Phillips, N. (2011). Strategies of alignment: Organizational identity management and strategic change a Bang & Olufsen. *Strategic Organization, 9*(2), 103–135.

Rego, A., Ribeiro, N., & Cunha, M. (2010). Perceptions of organizational virtuousness and happiness as predictors of organizational citizenship behaviors. *Journal of Business Ethics, 93*, 215–235. doi:10.1007/s10551-009-0197-7

Resick, C., Dickson, M., Mitchelson, J., Allison, L., & Clark, M. (2010). Team composition cognition, and effectiveness: Examining mental model similarity and accuracy. *Group Dynamics: Theory, Research, and Practice, 14*(2), 174–191. doi:10.1037/a0018444

Richards, R. (1976). James Gibson's passive theory of perception: A rejection of the doctrine of specific nerve energies. *Philosophy and Phenomenological Research, 37*(2), 218–233. doi:10.2307/2107193

Rolfsen, M., & Johansen, T. (2014). The silent practice: Sustainable self-managing teams in a Norwegian context. *Journal of Organizational Change Management, 27*(2), 175–187. doi:10.1108/JOCM-08-2012-0124

Rosen, C., Harris, K., & Kacmar, K. (2011). LMX, context perceptions, and performance: An uncertainty management perspective. *Journal of Management, 37*(3), 819–838. doi:10.1177/0149206310365727

Rosh, L., Offermann, L., & Van Diest, R. (2012). Too close for comfort? Distinguishing between team intimacy and team cohesion. *Human Resource Management Review, 22*(2), 116–127. doi:10.1016/j.hrmr.2011.11.004

Ross, C. (2014). The benefits of informal leadership. *Nurse Leader, 12*(5), 68–70. doi:10.1016/j.mnl.2014.01.015

Ruggieri, S., & Abbate, C. (2013). Leadership style, self-sacrifice, and team identification. *Social Behavior and Personality, 41*(7), 1171–1178. doi.org/10.2224/sbp.2013.41.7.1171

Salavati, A., Ahmadi, F., Sheikhesmaeili, S., & Mirzaei, M. (2011). Effects of Organizational Socialization (OS) on Organizational Citizenship Behavior (OCB). *Interdisciplinary Journal of Contemporary Research In Business, 3*(5), 395–410.

Saldaña, J. (2011). *Fundamentals of qualitative research.* New York, NY: Oxford University Press.

Sarangi, S., & Srivastava, R. (2012). Impact of organizational culture and communication on employee engagement: An investigation of Indian private banks. *South Asian Journal of Management, 19*(3), 18–33.

Schein, E. (2010). *Organizational culture and leadership.* Hoboken, NJ: Jossey-Bass.

Schilpzand, M., Martins, L., Kirkman, B., Lowe, K., & Chen, Z. (2013). The relationship between organizational justice and organizational citizenship behaviour: The role of cultural value orientations. *Management and Organization Review, 9*(2), 345–374. doi:10.1111/more.12014

Sendjaya, S., & Pekerti, A. (2010). Servant leadership as antecedent of trust in organizations. *Leadership & Organization Development Journal, 31*(7), 643–663. doi:10.1108/01437731011079673

Shim, M. (2010). Factors influencing child welfare employee's turnover: Focusing on organizational culture and climate. *Children and Youth Services Review, 32,* 847–856.

Shirey, M. (2013). Lewin's theory of planned change as a strategic resource. *The Journal of Nursing Administration, 43*(2), 69–72. doi:10.1097/NNA.0b013e31827f20a9

Simoes, P., & Esposito, M. (2014). Improving change management: How communication nature influences resistance to change. *Journal of Management Development, 33*(4), 324–341. doi:10.1108/JMD-05-2012-0058

Simonet, D., & Tett, R. (2013). Five perspectives on the leadership-management relationship: A competency-based evaluation and integration. *Journal of Leadership & Organizational Studies, 20*(2), 199–213. doi:10.1177/1548051812467205

Smart, M. (2005). *The role of informal leaders in organizations: The hidden organizational asset*. Moscow, ID: University of Idaho.

Smith, J. (2010). The rules of employee engagement: Management needs to take action to improve employee engagement. *Quality, 49*(6), 16.

Speitzer, G., De Janasz, S., & Quinn, R. (1999). Empowered to lead: The role of psychological empowerment in leadership. *Journal of Organizational Behavior, 20,* 511–526.

Stebbins, L., & Dent, E. (2011). Job satisfaction and organizational culture. *Journal of Applied Management and Entrepreneurship, 16*(1), 28–52.

Stoltzfus, K., Stohl, C., & Seibold, D. (2011). Managing organizational change: Paradoxical problems, solutions, and consequences. *Journal of Organizational Change Management, 24*(3), 349–367. doi:10.1108/09534811111132749

Stone, K. (2010). Kaizen teams: Integrated HRD practices for successful team building. *Advances in Developing Human Resources, 12*(1), 61–77. doi:10.1177/1523422310365333

Sy, T. (2010). What do you think of followers? Examining the content, structure, and consequences of implicit followership theories. *Organizational Behavior and Human Decision Processes, 113*(2), 73–84. doi:10.1016/j.obhdp.2010.06.001

Thomas, E., & Magilvy, J. (2011). Qualitative rigor or research validity in qualitative research. *Journal for Specialists in Pediatric Nursing, 16*(2), 151–155. doi:1 0.1111/j.1744-6155.2011.00283

Titrek, O., Polatcan, M., Zafer Gunes, D., & Sezen, G. (2014). The relationship among Emotional Intelligence (EQ), Organizational Justice (OJ), Organizational Citizenship Behaviour (OCB). *International Journal of Academic Research, 6*(1), 213–220. doi:10.7813/2075-4124.2014/6-1/B.30

Tonn, J. (2003). *Mary P. Follettt: Creating democracy, transforming management*. New Haven, CT: Yale University Press.

Turner, R., & Schabram, K. (2012). The bases of power revisited: An interpersonal perceptions perspective. *Journal of Organizational Psychology, 12*(1), 9–18.

Vakola, M. (2013). Multilevel readiness to organizational change: A conceptual approach. *Journal of Change Management, 13*(1), 96–109. doi:10.1080/14697 017.2013.768436 van der Voet, J. (2014). The effectiveness and specificity of change management in a public organization: Transformational leadership and a bureaucratic organizational structure. *European Management Journal, 32*(3), 373–382. doi. org/10.1016/j.emj.2013.10.001

van Knippenberg, D. (2011). Embodying who we are: Leader group prototypicality and leadership effectiveness. *The Leadership Quarterly, 22*, 1078–1091. doi:10.1016/j.leaqua.2011.09.004

Waite, R., McKinney, N., Smith-Glasgow, M., & Meloy, F. (2014). The embodiment of authentic leadership. *Journal of Professional Nursing, 30*(4), 282–291. doi:10.1016/j.profnurs.2013.11.004

Wang, D., & Hsieh, C. (2013). The effect of authentic leadership on employee trust and employee engagement. *Social Behavior and Personality: An International Journal, 41*(4), 613–624. doi.org/10.2224/sbp.2013.41.4.613

Wentzel-Larsen, T., Norekvål, T., Ulvik, B., Nygård, O., & Pripp, A. (2011). A proposed method to investigate reliability throughout a questionnaire. *BMC Medical Research Methodology, 11*(1), 137–143.

Wheelan, S., Davidson, B., & Tilin, F. (2003). Group development across time: Reality or illusion? *Small Group Research, 34*(2), 223–245.

Worley, C., & Mohrman, S. (2014). Is change management obsolete? *Organizational Dynamics, 43*(3), 214–224. doi:10.1016/j.orgdyn.2014.08.008

Yilmaz, K., & Altinkurt, Y. (2012). Relationship between the leadership behaviors, organizational justice, and organizational trust. *Faculty of Education Journal, 41*(1), 12–24.

Yin, R. (2014). *Case study research: Design and methods* (5th ed.). Thousand Oaks, CA: Sage Publications.

Yu-Chen, W. (2014). The benefits of organizational citizenship behavior for job performance and the moderating role of human capital. *International Journal of Business and Management, 9*(7), 87–99. doi:10.5539/ijbm.v9n7p87

Yukl, G. (2002). *Leadership in organizations* (5th ed.). Upper Saddle River, NJ: Prentice-Hall International.

Zhang, T., Avery, G., Bergsteiner, H., & More, E. (2014). The relationship between leadership paradigms and employee engagement. *Journal of Global Responsibility, 5*(1), 4–21. doi:10.1108/JGR-02-2014-0006

Index

Note: Page numbers in bold indicate a table on the corresponding page.

Printed in the United States
by Baker & Taylor Publisher Services